Loving, Launching, and Letting Go

For Debbie,
Blessings to you!
Vinita Kindu

Loving, Launching, and Letting Go

Preparing Your Nearly-Grown Children For Adulthood

VIRELLE KIDDER

FOREWORD BY GAIL MACDONALD

BROADMAN
&HOLMAN
PUBLISHERS

Nashville, Tennessee

Printed in the United States of America

Published by
Broadman & Holman Publishers
Nashville, Tennessee

Design: Steven Boyd

4261-86
0-8054-6186-8

Dewey Decimal Classification: 649
Subject Heading: Parenting \ Child Rearing
Library of Congress Card Catalog Number: 95-11384

Scripture quotations are from the Holy Bible, New International
Version, copyright © 1973, 1978, 1984 by International Bible
Society.

Library of Congress Cataloging-in-Publication Data
Kidder, Virelle
    Loving, launching, and letting go : preparing your nearly-grown
children for adulthood / by Virelle Kidder
        p. cm.
        Includes bibliographical references.
        ISBN 0-8054-6186-8 (pbk.)
        1. Parenting—Religious aspects—Christianity. 2. Child
rearing—Religious aspects—Christianity. 3. Parent and
teenager—Religious aspects—Christianity. 4. Adulthood—
Psychological aspects. 5. Kidder, Virelle. I. Title.
    BV4529.K53   1995
    248.845—dc20

    95-11384
    CIP
99 98 97 96 95 5 4 3 2 1

With loving appreciation to our parents,
Virginia Fransecky, and Robert and Lura Kidder,
who first held up the light we have followed,
and to my treasured husband, Steve,
who has taught our family what love is.
ॐ

Contents

Foreword

Someone has well noted that the two things we must give our children are roots and wings. In *Loving, Launching, and Letting Go*, Virelle Kidder gives us a clear sense of what it takes to offer both. From the day our children are born, we are teaching them how to live without us. Inch by inch, step by step, we want them to know we believe in their competency because we have given them the loving acceptance, affirmation, and skills that they need.

Life is full of letting-go moments. Releasing our children is only a part of many such occasions. It begins when we ourselves let go of our own roots and believe we can make it with God's help. Surely all of us remember our apprehensions on each child's first day at school, first night away from home, first ball game or recital, and first date.

Of course, the ultimate launching is when we let go at the moment of death. All other "letting gos" are preparing us for this one. Other releasings are giving us a chance to drill deep into our souls the reality that all of life is on loan and we are simply stewards of each thing, person, and breath God has shared with us.

It is comforting to me to realize that the Holy Family is an excellent model for us. Our Heavenly Father willingly "launched" His Son from a place of safety to a place of reviling and ultimate rejection. The Son let go of the comforts and privileges of heaven. Mary relinquished her rights over her body. Joseph let go of his reputation and his right to name his son and give him his seed. In each case, the response of letting go made future blessings possible. So it is with parenting.

Because I have known Virelle since her earliest parenting years, I have seen how these principles have worked in her home. I recall trials that would have made most of us whine, complain, and, yes, even quit. But Virelle pressed meaning into those challenges. She insisted that there was something to learn, something to deepen her love for Christ and her family, and even something to laugh about. Being a student of the Scriptures gave her coping tools that clearly show in her writing.

I also recall Virelle's ability to take others under her wing during those years, being there for them, and cheering as they attempted to master their own hurdles. It is this earnest desire to help others that runs through this book—practical, specific, measurable "handles" for a successful launch. I found the "Just Thinking" pages at the end of each chapter to be most helpful in integrating the suggestions given into conversations and family experience.

Virelle's honesty and vulnerability concerning her family's struggles makes readers aware that they are not alone in this uphill journey.

As one who has been reaping the joys of loving, launching, and letting go for many years now, I know that the principles of which Virelle speaks are true. I pray that this book will help all who read it to believe it is still possible to withstand the strains and pressures that accompany contemporary family life so that they, too, can have successful launches.

— Gail MacDonald

🐌

Acknowledgments

Writing a book is truly a team effort. I certainly couldn't have done this alone. My deep and heartfelt thanks go to many who have helped shepherd this book to completion.

To my amazing husband, Steve: You are second to none in humor, encouragement, service beyond what most husbands would even dream of, excellent but fearful editing, and making everything in my life fragrant with meaning. I love you!

To my dear children, Lauren and Mike, Amy and Keith, Bob and Theresa, and Dave, who are my heroes: Thank you for your faithful prayers and generous spirits that you always gave so freely. Special thanks to Dave for your genius and patience in helping me subdue my computer.

And to Brian, my "other son": Your encouragement and presence have meant a lot while our other children have been so far away.

To my mother go my special thanks for cheering loudly and long and for telling me all my life I should be a writer.

To Paul Hayford go my belated thanks for mentoring, training, and believing in me in my early ventures with writing.

Special thanks to all those who opened your hearts to me and allowed me to listen. All your stories should one day be told.

To Ron Haynes go my thanks for your great zeal and cheerfulness.

To the wonderful folks at Broadman & Holman who pray for their writers, thank you—especially to Vicki Crumpton, my editor, who knows how to dismantle and rebuild my writing with astonishing skill and good humor.

To Gail MacDonald for graciously adding your thoughts at the beginning of this book, but most of all, for lovingly investing yourself in me many years ago.

To all my dear friends who prayed and encouraged and didn't see me for months, I thank you and I love you.

Last and deepest of all, go my thanks to my Heavenly Father for trusting me to do this. It's all Yours.

ð‰

Introduction

*L*ast night was my first "ladies' night out" at our new church. At a beautiful restaurant overlooking the Hudson River, I met others who were also new to the church and unacquainted with one another.

The conversation went something like this: "Do you work outside your home? Are you married, and if so, do you have children? How old are they?" etc.

Fairly typical questions, but there was nothing typical about these women. Several had exciting careers, one was an opera singer, two had just returned from a cruise, and the cheery young woman who organized the event had recently survived two failed kidney transplants. No, not ordinary women at all; in fact, I found them quite extraordinary.

As the evening progressed, I mentioned that I was a writer working on a book on launching your kids into adulthood. Soon it seemed like everyone had something to say.

"Well, please hurry up!" one groaned. "I need it now! My kids are eleven and seventeen, and the next few years scare me!"

Another joined the conversation, "I can't picture life without my kids. I hope they never leave home. I hope they just get married and live with us forever."

"That's exactly what my son's doing next month," one lady added softly. I couldn't tell how she felt about it, and I marveled at her quiet acceptance.

"Forever? Are you kidding? I want my time back. I want time for myself for a change, even if it's just to read a book. And I really want some time with my husband, all by ourselves again, just to chase each other around the house if we want to. Now we have no privacy at all."

Suddenly a flashback made me chuckle. It was late one night, not that long ago, when a loud knock on our bedroom door was followed with, "Mom and Dad, are you in there? Why is this door locked? Can I come in and talk to you about something?" It's moments like these that bring parents to ask themselves how old they will be when the last one finally leaves home.

The ladies I met last night echoed the same concerns that Steve and I once had about the final stages of parenting—that often rugged process of loving, launching, and letting go.

Remember when you were a new parent and had all the answers? You and I were sure that launching our children would be a piece of cake. They would just float into adulthood in a flourish of outstanding accomplishments. And sometimes they do! Sometimes. Naturally, we all want our children to find happy, productive, and independent lifestyles. But the reality is they can need a lot of help getting there. You and I are wiser now, and this task looks tougher than we once thought.

What makes it tougher is that most parents have hidden fears about their offspring that have been brewing slowly for some time. With every small struggle, a worry took root.

- ❖ "What if they always do things this way?"
- ❖ "What if they never learn to stand on their own two feet?"
- ❖ "What if they don't do well in school and can't find a good career?"
- ❖ "What if they make poor choices and marry the wrong person, or get involved in a bad lifestyle?"
- ❖ "What if they can't make it and come back?"
- ❖ "Worse yet, what if they never leave ?"

You remember what their rooms looked like, or how they overslept four days in a row for their paper route, or nearly set the house on fire the first time they cooked dinner in your absence. It's hauntingly clear to parents that they're not finished raising them and yet the time's up! Some of these children will enter adulthood without knowing how to manage money, cook a decent meal, iron a shirt, or separate their laundry.

Parents worry, too, whether their young adults will ever remember to change the oil in their cars, or turn off the hose before it floods the basement, or pay their bills on time. All of this is small stuff compared to our real unspoken fears. What really scares us to death is whether they will try any of the really bad things we did at that age!

Launching your kids into adulthood is not for sissies! There's no right and wrong way to do it, no road map, no foolproof formula for success. The road ahead is totally unfamiliar to most of us, and the hurdles look higher than any we've tackled before. To make matters even tougher, the landscape is littered with families that didn't make it, with crippled relationships, and broken and distorted kids. You almost feel doomed to get wounded in the process.

That might be true. We were wounded ourselves, as were our children. Every one of us will carry certain marks on our heart from these years, but scars don't always make you look ugly. They can also enhance character and make you more beautiful.

The process of loving, launching, and letting go described on these pages can draw your family closer to God than any other time in your life. By learning to focus on what really matters most, your parenting will take on a clearer purpose, your prayer life will become simpler and more passionate, and your children will become truer testimonies of the grace, love, and power of God. It's a thrilling time ahead!

This book is the best gift I could give another parent on the road we've just traveled. It brings you the most significant help and encouragement that others gave us, including, how to know if your young adult is really ready to leave home, how to build closeness as a family, how to train teens to handle the nitty-gritties of daily living, ways to encourage a late bloomer, as well as how to avoid the worst mistakes parents can make. You will learn about the ways God helped our children and others create strength out of struggles and learn the hidden blessings of failure. Throughout the joys and unexpected challenges of these years, you will discover how to become parents who warm God's heart and raise kids who are hungry for your values.

Not to exclude the joys about to be yours, I hope to whet your appetite, as well, for the next unequaled chapter in your life: the empty nest! It is definitely better than you were once led to believe, and, yes, you are still young enough to enjoy it. Best of all, you will soon be amazed at the magnificent and quite surprising ways that God will flex His muscles in answering your prayers as your children's adult lives begin to unfold.

Loving, Launching and Letting Go is, for me, a kind of monument to God's amazing power and grace. Steve and I are humbled and grateful for these children who have become our best friends. I marvel at the awesome people they have become—men and women I truly admire. I have no doubt God will do the same and even more for you.

If you find yourself beginning these launching years full of anxiety, or if you're halfway through and feel like it's hopeless already, remember the story's not all told yet. But then, maybe I should tell you mine.

≈

Loving

CHAPTER ONE

"Imagine being done"
(and other helpful thoughts)

When the last guest left after Amy and Keith's wedding, Steve and I walked from room to empty room. "Is this *it?*" we asked aloud. "Are we really *done* raising our children?" It seemed so strange realizing that after a quarter century of loving and parenting four children, we had only each other once again. It felt nice but a little unnatural. Any moment now, I was certain I'd hear the thud of book bags in the front hall, followed by, "Hi, Mom, I'm home! What's for dinner?"

What a year it had been! Our three younger children, each seventeen months apart, all emerged into adulthood in one form or another and left the nest. We were somewhat prepared. Six years earlier our oldest daughter, Lauren, had begun the march to independence as she left for college, and subsequently, marriage. Her absence left a huge hole in our family that took months, if not years to adjust to. We all missed her terribly. Then, in what seemed like minutes, everyone was gone.

Amy was next in line, and, for her, leaving home meant the thrill of entering marriage and a whole new life with her handsome young husband, Keith, a professional chef. (What luck!) Having lived at home the longest, she had been standing on the edge of the nest anxiously flapping her wings for more than a year. Claiming God's promises in Jeremiah 29:11 and Psalm 37:4, Amy and Keith leaped into adult life full of faith and exhilaration.

For Dave, leaving meant facing heavy challenges as an industrial design major at college, playing lacrosse, and living away from home for the first time. Fitting a year's worth of toothpaste, shampoo, and laundry detergent into his meticulously packed boxes, he left behind two or three small tokens of his childhood laid carefully on his bed. Finding them nearly broke our hearts.

Our youngest son, Bob, chose early independence in a premature and bumpy liftoff from home, finishing his last year of high school and entering college in my husband's hometown to be nearer to a large extended family. Now we see more clearly God's hand in the matter and we are grateful it turned out well, but it was grueling at the time.

"Let's take stock," Steve said. "But first, let's *rest!*"

And rest we did! The house was almost musically quiet and unnaturally clean. A sense of hilarity came over me about five o'clock every night realizing that I really didn't *have* to cook anything if I didn't want to—which, in fact, I often didn't. We would order pizza or use two-for-one coupons for submarine sandwiches. We felt like newlyweds again.

Eating like that is fine for young lovers but disastrous for midlife bodies. Steve became my inspiration in an every-other-day exercise program. While he jogged miles and counted fat grams, I huffed and puffed around the block wondering how I could have deteriorated this much since my days as a cheerleader. My fat cells had enjoyed total freedom for decades.

Our new life alone fell easily along the outlines of habits we had developed over the years raising children. I used to bring Steve his coffee while he was shaving, and we would have a few minutes of relative quiet to talk over the coming day or review decisions about the children before the great slam of morning activity.

During the children's elementary and middle school years, we would read Bible stories or a chapter of Proverbs a day with them while waiting for the school bus. Life was hectic enough then, but when high school years began, the door to easy morning devotions swung shut. We were fortunate to squeeze in hugs and a quick prayer. Opportunities for teaching and sharing openly about God's Word became as rare as rubies.

Rarer still in those days was time alone together. Now we relish a morning walk with coffee, time for devotions together, and even time to exercise before a busy day. Some of our most personal sharing times have begun in the morning and continued throughout the day.

TRUSTING THE LORD

Raising our children has not been easy—joyful and rewarding in many ways, yes, but we've also had our share of heartbreak. We know there will be other challenges ahead, but at this time of repose, we relish the thought of being, for all practical purposes, *done.* The outcome is in the Lord's hands and our children's wills. God is still in charge, but He may yet have surprises for us with our offspring.

Looking back over the span of years and memories in this green split-level house under the tall pines, I know I often felt a sense of failure as a mother and a wife. There was seldom enough of me to meet everyone's needs. I could be cranky, selfish, and unreasonable, as my children sometimes were. I have asked the Lord to erase any hurtful memories I may have caused them, even those I was unaware of at the time. (Are there any seasoned parents who don't live with at least some stinging flashbacks when they were their own worst nightmare? I don't know any.)

But there were good things that happened here, too—real, hard, true things like forgiveness and acceptance and trusting God for the unknown and the very frightening times. There was laughter and frivolity, as well as sadness—deep as joy—and renewal like the morning sun. God lived here in our home these many years, holding our hearts in the palm of His hand. He carried us all, at times, like lambs on His shoulder.

Today there are miracles we give God total credit for: All four children emerged with their faith in Christ tested but still intact, and they are our very good friends. Two wonderful sons-in-law, Michael and Keith, and a new daughter-in-law, Theresa, have been added to our family. We wouldn't trade them for the entire New York State lottery jackpot. They each love the Lord Jesus and our daughters and son. What could be better than that? Now I am praying for one more special daughter-in-law whom we haven't met yet!

BUILDING ON A SURE FOUNDATION

When I was nineteen, I studied and traveled in Europe for a summer using a little money I had inherited from my grandfather. Perhaps because it sounded like a safe program, my mother let me go. More the opposite, it was twelve weeks full of risk, thrills, and adventure. I also learned more Spanish than I had in five previous years of study and a lot about life. Strangely, it was a little thing I learned that stayed with me to this day.

One day near the end of the summer, my roommate invited four or five of us to come to her home in Holland, near Rotterdam, for a visit before returning to college. The fact that we were nearly penniless by now made no difference. Ah, youth! We simply advertised in our five combined languages on the university bulletin board that we needed a ride to Paris. We found one and in a big Mercedes at that. Then we pooled our money for train tickets to the Netherlands where my friend's parents were waiting for us. Imagine our surprise as they drove us to their home—a beautiful mansion on a private lake! It felt like heaven!

What a welcome relief a home-cooked meal and a warm, clean bed were! Her parents made us feel like family. But the first night there, I learned something amazing.

Everything in the Netherlands is built on sand! No matter how big or beautiful the house, when a truck goes by, the whole house shakes! It shook so often that night that I could hardly sleep. I imagined what it might do in an electric storm like the ones we had at home off the Great Lakes. Very unsettling, to say the least!

The point being made is simple. In order to provide an unshakable foundation from which to launch our children into their adult lives, our homes need to be built on the bedrock of truth found in Jesus Christ and the whole of His Word, the strength of His promises, and the height and depth of His love. No matter how wonderful other things may appear to be, anything less is risky at best. Just like the simple illustration Jesus gave of the two men who built their homes, one on the rock and the other on the sand, when the storms of life hit both houses, the one on the rock never even quivered (see Matt. 7:24–27).

We had storms that proved God's faithfulness. I'm certain you have, too. Even in our darkest times when our children experienced suffering, when our marriage and our faith were stretched almost beyond our own ability to endure, God was always strong for us. He will be equally faithful to you, too. The one great underpinning of the Christian home that gives it such unmatched strength and resilience is the foundational knowledge of the love of God in the Person of His Son Jesus

Christ. Parents who allow that love to control them will release children who carry His likeness to the next generation.

THE VALUE OF BEING REAL

Accepting our children for who they are and who God wants them to become is a necessary step toward a successful launch. Regardless of how many wonderful outside influences a young adult may have, parents are still God's first choice to prepare them for their adult lives. Steve and I raised not ideal children, but *real* people, whom we know very well by now—flaws and all—and love them deeply. They also know their parents as real people, too, who have suffered along with them, grown and matured along with them, and are very far from perfect. We feel an overriding sense of gratefulness to God for His unfailing love and power to create, renew, and rebuild life.

FINDING A LIFELINE

With any problem, try as we may, it seems impossible to figure out what God is doing. What good could come out of this hurtful problem at school, this foolish mistake, or even this delay in plans? But God works silently on the infrastructure of our homes and every life in them. Even though He doesn't always let us in on His purposes, He makes strong promises to families and keeps them. We may need to claim those promises a hundred times a day, holding onto them like a lifeline. By allowing God freedom, giving Him lordship over every area of this business of raising a family, He will make good on every promise we claim, becoming the unshakable foundation of our home. He is the Master Builder and the Chief Cornerstone all in one, the Architect of a godly heritage, the Giver of dreams, the one true Father whose love calls and compels every lost child until they are safely home at last.

In my earlier book, *Mothering Upstream: Help, Encouragement and Vision from a Mother Who Has Been There*, I had a strong desire to help other mothers over some of the same hurdles I encountered. There were loads of them—more than I could have covered in several volumes. (But what mother has time to read several volumes?) So, I chose those struggles that loomed largest in my memory bank. In the writing process, I grew to love the reader very much. I have since met "her" in many different faces and places and our real friendship has grown.

The next few years following the writing of that book found me exceptionally busy finishing along with Steve the surprisingly bumpy process of "getting these calves across the stream." Everything else became secondary. We found the last few years of raising and releasing our children to be the most emotionally strenuous, perplexing, and faith-stretching of all. There seemed no end to the amount of wisdom we needed to launch kids into adulthood, as well as patience, financial genius, humor, and sympathy. No nerves were left unstretched. Loving, launching, and letting go are not unlike labor and delivery; the biggest strain and life-giving efforts are often the grand finale.

"The reason it's so difficult," quips my wise friend Lorraine, "is that you'd never want to let go of them unless you couldn't stand the strain any longer! God has His ways of making letting go easier!"

That's what this book is about, dear friend. It's all about God's magnificent grace in helping you as a perplexed parent, feeling perhaps worn-out and drained, to find new hope, surprising rest, release, and power to take you through this last stage of parenting and to launch your children into adulthood in His keeping.

You will find all the promises of God to be true in your home as well as mine. You will marvel at all God will do in answer to your prayers, not immediately, perhaps; but just as certainly as you are you, and I am myself, He is the great "I AM" and He will answer.

May this book and the warmth of His hand make your road a little easier. The Lord be with you.

JUST THINKING

Why not take a few minutes with your spouse and "take stock" like we did? List the ages of your children and count the precious months left with each one. Now, write down the best qualities you see in each child. Take a moment to thank God for placing them there.

Next, talk about the biggest needs still waiting to be filled in each young life. Is it loneliness, direction, self-esteem, common sense, self-discipline? Ask God to help you become an even more sensitive parent, opening up your awareness to His priorities.

Last, talk honestly about the biggest struggles you face in the whole process of releasing your children into adulthood. Share the worries that have taken root over the years. Confess these things to God in prayer and ask His help while there is still time.

≈

CHAPTER TWO

Countdown to launch: four ways to know if they're ready to leave home

Joe Cool (or Josephine). See him smile. Your son is ready to leave home. He looks great, smells great, acts suave and mature, spends money like an executive, and talks like a pro. His bags are packed meticulously; he even opted for no TV and the smaller stereo for his dorm room. Look at that impressive schedule book he keeps, just like his dad. Junior has finally arrived. Everyone is impressed. But wait a minute. Mom and Dad look concerned—in fact, more like worried.

Behind all the laughter and last-minute lightheartedness, they see a different picture. They know their wonderful son very well. In spite of how much they love him, they also know his shortcomings—how he leaves the iron on every morning before school (thank God for the new automatic shut-off iron Mom bought him for college), regularly skips breakfast but grabs a Coke and a candy bar just before lunch, and chronically forgets to pay his little brothers the money he borrows. Dad winces at the memory of his new top coat Junior borrowed for a special formal dinner date and left at the restaurant. The list is endless, but when the future looks so bright, why drag up the past? After all, who has a perfect child?

It would seem there is no way to know when your child is ready to leave home. If only there were some magical checklist for parents to follow. How do parents know if they're doing too much for their children? Love should have no limits, right?

KNOW WHAT YOU'RE AIMING AT

We all know how confusing raising children can be. So many situations are new and often complex, and it doesn't get any easier as our children get older. The few years that precede teenagers leaving home present so many choices and challenges, some parents give up and just say a blanket yes or no to everything. To alleviate both extremes, it helps to know what you're aiming at during these years.

In my earlier book, *Mothering Upstream,* I talked about the three most important things to rearing our children: honesty, obedience, and kindness. Other families might have different priorities, but those worked for us and helped us keep from coming unglued over unimportant issues.

Similarly, the releasing process needs parameters, as well. What matters most?

Maybe you're thinking, *I really want them to be happy with who they are and make good choices.* Still others will be more concerned with economics and want to make certain their son or daughter prepares well for a high-paying career. Many parents simply respond loudly, "I just want them to find something they want to do and do it!"

FOUR WAYS TO KNOW IF THEY'RE READY

There may not be a magic formula for ensuring success, but there are four pretty accurate ways to measure our children's readiness to live on their own. They are areas of maturity that parents can aim at as the countdown to launch progresses. These areas have nothing to do with outward appearances or academic achievement, rather they are indicators of character, wisdom, and spiritual maturity. As you look at the young adults in your own home, consider these four things:

1. Are they able to stand on their own two feet without your continual help?

2. Do they demonstrate some degree of wisdom and maturity in their lifestyles and decision making?

3. Can they maintain healthy relationships both within and without the home?

4. Of chief importance to Christian parents, do they have an authentic walk with God that will impact every other relationship?

Willingness to accept responsibility, handle life's challenges, work hard, and become self-supporting all stem from these four basic areas. Knowing what we are aiming at eliminates a lot of foolish worry and unnecessary conflict. It can also cause us to recognize problems brewing before they get too big to handle. Let's take a look at each of these target areas and a few practical tips to help you get there.

1. Standing on Their Own

From the time their children are small, most good parents make an effort to teach them how to handle life at their current level. They teach their children to take care of an increasing number of tasks on their own: from cleaning their room, to feeding the dog, to earning money for some of their own special wants or needs.

But somehow, the teenage years hit and kids seem to forget all that wonderful responsibility they learned. Worse yet, by lifting them over every small hurdle with our instant help and solutions, we communicate doubt over their ability to become capable adults.

I don't know if you have ever found yourself in the trap of doing far too much for your children, but it's easy to do. In fact, it can be easier than making our young people become responsible for themselves. In the long run, it's a bad way to live; it trains our teens to see their parents less as friends and counselors and more as people whose job it is to do things for them. Not a healthy choice.

I'll never forget the day I resigned as a mom. I still had three older teenagers at home with busy, demanding lives which somehow spilled over onto mine quite frequently. I admit I was overly accommodating. I guess I just assumed one day my son or daughter would come downstairs and say, "Don't worry, Mom, I'll take care of those errands for you while I'm out. And never mind, I've already ironed my shirt for the concert tonight and returned those tapes to the video rental store."

Steve dreamed of hearing, "Say, Dad, could you just check over my income tax statement. I finished it last night. Oh, and by the way, I put some gas in your car on my way home from practice. Thought you might need it full today for your trip."

In spite of all the wonderful things our children said and did, those words never came out of anyone's mouth. And then I resigned.

I'm not sure what led to the explosion that day. It was a Sunday afternoon and everyone was relaxing after dinner. Everyone, that is, except me. I was in the kitchen feeling sorry for myself. Mentally I kicked through the rubble of my plans to relax as each person's perceived needs piled up around mine. There was no time left for me. I jammed the last glass in the dishwasher and slammed it shut so hard that I heard the tinkle of broken glass, or rather, several broken glasses.

"Hey, Mom, what's come over you?" came a voice from the next room.

"I *quit!* That's what's come over me!" I shouted back and made no effort to fight the tears as I ran up to my room and searched for a pen and paper.

Later, we called it a "Four-Glass Resignation." It may have been a little corny, but it worked. Big red letters on a yellow legal pad said something like this:

To My Children:

I hereby resign as your mother. I am no longer your cook, laundress, maid, chauffeur, or banker.

You are now completely responsible for your-selves, and I am solely and completely your father's girlfriend.

I will always be available if you need a friend or counselor.

Effective immediately.

Mom

There was a quiet you could feel as I posted the declaration of my emancipation on the refrigerator. The relief for me was immediate, and Steve winked his approval at having me back as just his girlfriend.

One of my kids read it out loud and added, "Isn't this going a bit far?"

"Hey, it's fine with me," said another.

"No problem here," shrugged the third. "I never ask for anything anyway."

But my teens didn't like it much when they had to make their own dinner, or figure out their own transportation. It was difficult not to spring into action when someone lost a favorite sweater, needed a lunch made fast, or discovered a school event conflicted with a dentist appointment. I had to resist the strong urge to "fix" everyone's problems.

On the positive side, it didn't take long at all for change to occur. My "resignation" increased respect and appreciation for everyone's time and energies, not just mine. It was a pleasant transition when my teenagers recognized themselves as young adults who could manage very nicely on their own.

Taking responsibility for themselves should include things like this:

Taking care of all their personal needs on a daily basis without leaving behind them a trail ten feet wide. This includes personal grooming, laundry, preparing their own breakfasts, lunches, and occasionally dinners, keeping their belongings in order so as not to infringe on other people's space, and just generally managing their own "maintenance."

When my friend Mary's twenty-year-old son moved back home to finish college, she promptly bought him a laundry hamper. Then she thought, "Why am I buying only one?" Soon, the four teenagers still living at home learned to manage their laundry, too. Mary gained hours to do other things.

Handling money responsibly. If your son or daughter is always asking you for cash when he has some source of income, there's a problem. Teach him how to use money for giving to the Lord, setting aside savings for college or future needs, and for the extra things he wants that are beyond your budget. One parent I know taught his teens to keep a notebook and record all spending. He never had to say much when they discovered how many of their own dollars were disappearing into fast-food restaurants.

Learning to manage a checking account along with the responsibility of a part-time job is wonderful preparation for life away from home. Some parents also allow their teenagers a credit card of their own during this "training period" with the understanding that the first month they are unable to pay their balance in full, the card is destroyed. I admire a young person who can handle this responsibility. Frankly, I think the risk is greater than the value.

Completing required tasks without prodding. It's alarming how many parents never trained their children to enjoy work.

They used work as a punishment or something to be endured. By the time your children are preparing to leave home, it becomes very clear that success comes more often to the hard worker than the brilliantly talented. If you are having a hard time enlisting the efforts of your busy young person around the house, try linking privileges with faithful performance of duties through the use of contracts. It may seem elementary now, but it's better than arguing. When kids sign an agreement, they learn that nothing is automatic in adult life. When we work hard, we get paid, and we achieve results. It's as simple as that.

2. Showing Wisdom

When I was a little girl, occasionally I'd hear of an older woman with a funny name like "Prudence" or "Prudy" for short. I always felt sorry for her growing up with a name that sounded like something unpleasant to me, like prunes. Names like that, I figured, should be outlawed. Of course, that was a little strange itself coming from someone with a name like Virelle. (I was always relieved my name didn't really mean anything. It was just a combination of my parents' names, Virginia and Russell.)

Then one day many years later, I came across the word prudence in Proverbs 8:12, "I, wisdom, dwell together with *prudence*; I possess knowledge and discretion." Thinking it must have some weighty meaning if God considered it a virtue, I looked it up. Webster's dictionary equates prudence with wisdom in action, calling it "wisdom shown in the exercise of reason, forethought, and self-control."[1] All in all, a first-rate quality for anyone to have.

Thereafter, I fell in love with the word *prudence*, finding it fragrant with meaning related to the Christlike life. Now I wouldn't mind a bit having a name like that. Neither would I worry too much about releasing a prudent son or daughter into their adult lives, would you?

Prudence is like having a protective coating on the inside of your life that seals in the good things and seals out the bad. It's a God-inspired lens through which to view the world, its temptations and challenges. Prudence kicks you in the pants when you feel like sloughing off, and it slows you down when you run ahead of God. It squirrels away a little for tomorrow's needs or today's kindness. Prudence isn't faith, but rather the result of a life trained by faith. It is strength and foresight becoming one—something we pray will be formed in our child's life from the love and time we've poured in and the shaping God has required.

Wisdom is a good thing to pray for every day in your own life, your husband's or wife's, your children's lives as well as those of their future mates. Wisdom results when God, out of His deep generosity, enables us to look at life from His point of view. Would we seek any other?

Wise Guys (and Gals)

Some of the ways wisdom might be evidenced in your young adults are:

- ❖ doing the right thing when no one is looking, or when it is personally inconvenient to do so,
- ❖ handling an emergency when no parent is available and making excellent decisions,
- ❖ explaining politely to a teacher why they take a different point of view based on their faith,
- ❖ controlling their tempers when someone else was losing theirs,
- ❖ making a carefully thought-out, prayed-through decision,
- ❖ resisting temptation of all sorts.

"If any of you lacks wisdom, he should ask God who gives generously to all without finding fault, and it will be given to him" (James 1:5). If you want more wisdom for those around you, pray to demonstrate it more yourself, for wisdom finds its reflection in others.

Why not share with your teen the times you've already seen him or her display this kind of wisdom? Let him know how highly valued it is both to you and to God. Talk about the areas in his life where you'd like to see him exercise more wisdom before he is ready to leave home. It will help you both know what you're aiming at.

Be careful to be helpful, not critical. It's far better at this stage to get on his team, encouraging him to exercise the kind of mature wisdom that you know will lead to making wise choices. Pray for the courage to see him through to completion. It's worth praying for.

3. Maintaining Healthy Relationships

I wish I could remember where I heard it or read it, but one day I came across the phrase, "Secrets are to sickness as openness is to wholeness," and I stopped and repeated it aloud several times until it sunk in deeply. Aren't we all ashamed of the times when we've contained some relationship or activity under the covering of secrecy? Pretty soon, we've spun a web of lies and self-deception that warped all our relationships. When a parent senses secrecy in a teen, it's cause for concern. Red flags might be withdrawal from the family at meal times, long private phone conversations, or showing very little interest communicating what she is up to or where she's been.

Even the sweetest teens can get innocently caught in a web of secrecy. When parents sense it happening, it may require loving confrontation to help their young person become free from whatever unhealthy activities, thought patterns, or relationships have begun to hold him down. It's such a comfort to know we're not alone in this. God desires the best for all His children, and He parents along with us at our request.

Once when our eldest daughter was a senior in high school, I think she held the record for carrying a heavy load of responsibility. We had tremendous respect for the high standards she had set for herself, but when she began to date a very nice boy one year younger than she, we felt concern over his lack of communication with adults. Somehow, Steve and I never felt he was being totally straight with us. After dating awhile, our normally bubbly and open daughter became almost guarded in what she said to us. Because she had helped this young man become a Christian and attend youth group at our church, most of their dates revolved around that, so we decided to just trust her judgment and pray.

Not long after the school year began, Steve and I went to a weekend conference and left Lauren in charge of her thirteen-year-old sister and two younger brothers. We were only a few hours away, and left with only one instruction: She'd have to forego youth group that night because we wanted her to be at home.

About ten o'clock that night we called home to see how things were going, and Amy answered. Amy absolutely couldn't lie "successfully," and when we asked why Lauren didn't come to the phone, she blurted out, "Don't be mad at her, Mom. She was so sad to miss the big youth group hayride, I convinced her to go. I knew I could take care of things!"

I think we were more surprised than angry. This kind of behavior was so unlike either of the girls at that age, but we hadn't counted on God's handling it for us.

When Lauren drove away in the old green Chrysler, she knew it was wrong, but somehow justified her judgment because her boyfriend was a really new Christian and she felt "responsible" to get him to youth group. After she picked him up, they drove quite a distance to meet the group at a farm up in the Helderberg mountains.

It was a dark, cold October night and the road was unfamiliar. If Lauren felt a little uneasy during the hayride and devotions around the bonfire, she must have felt absolutely sick when it was time to leave as she reached in her pocket for the car keys and discovered they were gone. For nearly an hour the whole youth group and their leaders searched the hay wagons by flashlight until someone found her keys.

Nervously, Lauren and her boyfriend drove down the mountain and soon became totally lost. Later we realized they drove crisscross back and forth on the wrong side of the mountain searching for the right road home. It was another hour later before she pulled safely in our driveway and sputtered to a stop, out of gas.

When Steve and I heard the story the next night, we were tremendously relieved and thankful to know Lauren was all right but naturally disappointed over her bad choices. God had protected her but made the path of disobedience miserable. As she sat on the piano bench describing the whole ordeal, red-nosed and sobbing, Lauren responded with real openness to her dad's loving confrontation about the effect her new boyfriend was having on her.

"Give yourself some time without this relationship, honey," he said. "If it's right, he'll still be there later." Lauren agreed, and health and wholeness were transfused back into our relationship. Both she and Amy had their "wings clipped" for a couple of weeks, just as a reminder to everyone that the truth pays off, but secrecy boxes you in. (Just a word of caution: if discipline is needed after restoring openness with your teen, be gentle. It's not time to play "the heavy," but rather to foster trust and mutual respect whenever possible.)

If you can feel real openness from your older teen, you are well on the way to peace of mind when he or she leaves home. But if not, I would urge you to find a quiet, non-threatening time and place to ask your young adult if he or she is completely satisfied with the quality of his friendships, the effect they have on him, and if he feels closer to God or farther from Him when in the company of his most intimate friends. The manner in which you speak about this should demonstrate the kind of courtesy, love, and openness you want to receive from your son or daughter.

4. Trusting God on Their Own

There is no greater peace for parents than to discover their young adult has a real relationship with God on his own. When they dig for answers in Scripture, pray long and hard about their choices for the future, and desire God's best more than a quick or attractive solution to things, you have much to rejoice over. It's time to "back up, pray up, and shut up," as author Jan Silvious puts it. God is in the driver's seat with your child and it's time to let go.

That's easier said than done. "Most of us," said Oswald Chambers, "are so noisy in our instruction of others that God can't get anywhere near them."[2] We really aren't the Holy Spirit's personal representative to our children that we imagine ourselves to be, and it only takes a few colossal mistakes to reveal it. Do you and I really want to risk it? I would rather become a better cheerleader than a coach at this point. Frankly, most of us could use a few more cheerleaders and a few less coaches in our lives.

Coaches' comments cut the air like this:

- ❖ "When are you going to get busy and get those applications out?"
- ❖ "Do I have to do everything for you?"
- ❖ "You really should have asked my opinion before you did that."

Cheerleaders, on the other hand, say things like this:

- ❖ "I know you'll be able to make the right decision about college. I have a lot of confidence in you."

❖ "I'm certain you will know when God opens the right door for you."

❖ "Mom and I are really pleased with the way you've managed your tough schedule this year."

❖ "What's your honest opinion on . . . ?"

❖ "Can you give me your advice about something? I need someone to help me think through a difficult decision."

What a compliment to a teenager when parents actually respect his opinion and allow him the privilege of making important decisions the way God does—without reminding him of past mistakes. Doesn't it feel great to know we can approach our Heavenly Father for the wisdom to make tough decisions without Him bringing up the past? What a great model for us as parents of teens teetering on the edge of the nest called "home."

Just Thinking

Parents, take a few moments and list everything you regularly do to help your young person. Now ask yourselves which things you are doing that might actually inhibit his ability to live on his own one day. Talk with your teenager about systematically transferring those responsibilities back to him or her.

Next, decide which are the most important qualities your son or daughter should have prior to leaving home, and then review the list with him. Ask him how he feels he's doing. Now ask yourself if you are more often a coach or a cheerleader. Whose team would you like to play on if you were seventeen or eighteen?

CHAPTER THREE

God's clock seems slow: strategies to encourage a late bloomer

God's time is never wrong,
  Never too fast nor too slow,
  The planets move to its steady pace
  As the centuries come and go.
  Stars rise and set by that time,
  The punctual comets come back
  With never a second's variance,
  From the round of their viewless track.
  Men space their years by the sun,
  And reckon their months by the moon,
  Which never arrive too late
  And never depart too soon.
  Let us set our clocks by God's,
  And order our lives by His ways,
  And nothing can come and nothing can go
  Too soon or too late in our day.
            – Annie Johnson Flint[1]

———

Over the years I've learned a few lessons about God's timing: chiefly, that He's setting His watch by a different clock than mine. And although He may make us wait a long time, God loves to "wow" us with His surprises, His huge "over-anwers" to our long-term deepest prayers. He loves to have His children look only to Him for answers, not to their own wits. And when He answers, He does so in a manner that will take your breath away. That's worth waiting for.

How wonderful it would be if we could simply trust God's timing perfectly in our children's lives, or even our own, for that matter. From the time their children are born, most parents have at least some concern as to whether or not they are learning, doing things, and developing "on schedule." The concern is no less intense with young adults under our roof; in fact, it can be even more pronounced, especially when they seem to be lagging behind everyone else their age socially, emotionally, physically, or intellectually.

ASPECTS OF A LATE BLOOMER

My mother loves to tell the story of her older brother, Jerome. He was so small in high school that his nickname was "Pony." Almost overnight the summer of his senior year, he grew about a foot to an imposing six-foot-three or so. I always knew my Uncle Jerry as a big, tall, huggable person whose smile and wit lit up my world. He could have been considered a late bloomer in other ways, as well. After pursuing an art career at Yale, he floundered personally and professionally until his business took off with his creative management. He knew how to believe in people and inspire them to achieve their own greatest potential, whether late or early. It didn't matter.

Growth Levels

Physical growth is one thing, but there other types of maturity that can be even more perplexing for parents. "How do I answer people," confided a friend to me one day, "when they want to know where my daughter will go to school next year? How can I tell them we're just hoping she'll graduate on time? It's so humiliating for her. She has no plans for next year at all."

Cooperating with God

One mother I know, a single mom and a godly and practical woman, shared her perspective with me. "I realized one day that my son was about two years behind his friends in everything. It wasn't fair to criticize him for it; that's just the way God made him. I could either cooperate with God and wait two years or make my son's and my life miserable. I chose to cooperate with God, and I'm glad I did." Today she enjoys a close relationship with her son and his wife and marvels at the way he matured. Had she nagged and complained and compared him to his friends or siblings, she could have dismantled brick by brick all the strength God was building slowly into his life.

It's unbelievably difficult for the parents of a late bloomer to pretend to be interested in someone else's young genius and his or her choice between full scholarships at Princeton or Berkeley. How insensitive others can be as they chirp on and on about their child's successes in the company of these parents. Inwardly their hearts are breaking and they're worried sick that their child may never make it in life, never find a good career, miss the boat meeting the right person, or never find satisfaction in an independent lifestyle. Frankly, it's scary to think that a child may never leave home! We've all known families whose forty-year-old son or daughter never left! No one wants to parent forever.

Platitudes won't do. It's no use saying, "Oh, don't worry. Suzy's just shy, that's all. She'll find her niche one day." To the parent whose child is the last one off the starting block, that translates as, "Suzy's way behind. You just better pray she catches up with everyone else!"

I find it hard to believe that God is as worried about late bloomers as we are. Our vision is so distorted just by our "earthlyness." We need a closer walk with Him and a saturation with His Word to gain perspective.

The Waiting Process

Elisa Morgan, president of Mothers of Preschoolers (M.O.P.S.) International and author of *I'm Tired of Waiting,* writes about the waiting process this way:

> Cooperating with our Gardener means enduring the pruning process. This takes faith. We cringe at the sight of God's clippers. Snip. Snip. Snip. "Not that part!" we call. "Not so short!" we beg. "Please leave that long one intact," we bargain.
>
> While you're waiting, delight in what God is growing. Send your roots deep and drink from the streams of His living Word.
>
> Whether in a Dixie cup or in the garden of our lives, seeds grow in the dark over a long period of time. Resist the urge to dig them up. While you're waiting for your crop to come in, cooperate with the Gardener.[2]

It's hard to endure the pruning process when it's your son or daughter who is being pruned. Some of the seeds of maturity and even greatness may remain a long time in the dark. It may seem that nothing is happening in your young adult's life. Why doesn't he get moving? Why can't he decide on a career or stick with a job? Why the restlessness and lack of motivation?

As parents we are so impatient! We want flowers now! But the Master Gardener is never impatient. He is willing to wait for the end result. He knows real beauty is never achieved in a hurry.

Finding Strength and Managing Weakness

At Home

One of the best ways to prepare our children for their adult lives is to affirm their talents and strengths from the moment they begin to display them. If we didn't point out their talents at home, it may take them years to realize them on their own. (Remember: It's never too late to begin.) Perhaps you remember saying things like this to your children:

"You are so tactful and pleasant on the phone. I hope one day you are in lots of contact with people."

"That's a beautiful job you did on the lawn (or whatever). Have you ever thought about becoming a landscape architect?"

"This woodworking project looks almost professional. You are very talented with your hands."

"This is very well written. Have you ever thought of becoming an English teacher or a writer?" (My mother's favorite line.)

"How did you manage to save so much money from your summer job? I'm amazed at your ability to handle money so well at your age." (I wish we had said more of this!)

At School

If the home can point out a child's strengths, so can the school environment. I remember well a girl with whom I went to high school who stuttered badly, but when her teacher encouraged her to sing in the school choir, she discovered her stuttering was completely gone when she sang. She began singing solos in her sensitive, beautiful voice, and it changed her life dramatically. Encourage your children to explore many different areas of interest in school and extracurricular activities. It's generally true that the busier teenagers are, the happier they are.

But school can also deliver harmful blows to a young person's self-esteem by revealing areas of weakness and failure in very public ways. A parent's words of encouragement can be drowned out by the thundering message inside their heads, "You're a failure! You're no good at math, or reading, or sports! You're no good at anything!"

We all have weaknesses in different areas, and a parent's role isn't to deny the problem, but to help our young person manage or cope with these areas of personal weakness. Everyone has something they're not good at. I was never very athletic. In fact, I can remember the sting of being the last one picked for kickball or soccer in gym, but I learned I had a loud yell and boundless enthusiasm for others in sports, so I worked hard to become a cheerleader, instead. It's a great relief when we realize we don't have to be perfect at everything to be happy and complete.

If your son or daughter is artistically talented but also colorblind like our son Dave, help him focus his talent in areas that are not dependent on color. Dave is now a senior industrial design student and accomplishes most of his design work in black and white or neutral tones.

Or perhaps you have a kid who can whip up dinner for the whole family with whatever is in the house and make it taste spectacular, but at school he struggles with reading. Buy him a small computer and a set of his own cooking tools and encourage him to train at the Culinary Institute of America like my son-in-law's parents did. Now he's a well-respected chef in his own right, who memorizes recipes with little effort and expresses his love for others through cooking.

SUGGESTIONS FOR PARENTS

Encourage Your Children

Our aim for our children should not be to force them into the mold we have created for them, but rather to help them find God's design for their lives. He built them with certain strengths and certain weaknesses. Both are necessary for becoming a balanced human being.

In their book *Five Cries of Parents*, Merton and Irene Strommen underscore the importance of parental encouragement but not control in helping young people find their niche: "Adolescents have a need to achieve, to excel in a tangible way. . . .To know one does well in an activity vastly enhances one's sense of self-esteem. The parent's task is to help the adolescent discover his or her 'special gift' and then affirm each hesitant effort to develop this ability."[3]

There are plenty of ways to help your young adult zero in on his or her particular bent.

❖ Help him or her find a way to work with or spend time with others in the occupation he's interested in. Does he love animals? Work part-time at a veterinary clinic. Gifted in photography perhaps? Sign up for a weekend or evening course at a community college. Become the family photographer or even the school or church photographer.

❖ Would your son or daughter like to be a teacher? Why not assist a Sunday School teacher, or even take on teaching a children's class themselves? Young teens who baby-sit regularly often continue their studies in early childhood education to see if careers in that area appeal to them. The training alone is valuable later in their adult lives.

❖ I know a young woman who loves science, but discovered a nursing career wasn't for her. She recently began talking to people in environmental science professions—an excellent way to learn what it's really like to work in that field.

* There are services available in most larger communities to help your young adult discover, through a series of interviews and questionnaires, which careers he or she is best suited for. These may be expensive for some families, so I mention them last, but it can be very encouraging for young people to find how many career opportunities are open to them in fields they already enjoy. I knew a young man who liked both languages and business. Even though they seemed nearly opposite careers to him, he discovered ways to use his talents both in short-term missions and in the international business community. Eureka!

Prize Their Uniqueness

It's almost universally true that your second child will never follow the same timetable as the first, neither will the third follow in the footsteps of the second, and so on. What baffles us as parents is that we come to expect everyone to do everything in the same way and worry when they don't. Far more important than our children following our best plans for them is helping them discover God's unique and wonderful plan for their lives.

Many years ago in Baltimore when I was both a young mother and a brand new Christian, I was worried about what God's plan for my life might be. It's not uncommon to wonder if God will require some supreme and terrible sacrifice in your life in order to please Him. I wanted His will, but I was really afraid of what it might be. Then one day I spoke with an elderly lady who was well known in the area as a Bible teacher. I'll never forget her answer, as it has guided me through much of my life.

"Do you remember the story of Abraham's search for a wife for his son, Isaac?" she asked me one day over the phone.

"Not really," I admitted. At the time I frankly knew very little of Abraham or anyone else in the Bible.

"Well, you'll like it. It's a great love story. Old Abraham sent his most faithful servant to his homeland to find the woman God had chosen for Isaac. The servant, full of uncertainty over how he would recognize the girl, prayed that God would direct him by an exact set of circumstances that would be so unusual as to be almost impossible unless God had engineered it.

"When the servant arrived at Abraham's homeland, the very first person he met was the beautiful young woman, Rebekah. She did exactly as Abraham's servant prayed she would: She offered him a drink from the well and offered to water his camels. With that, the servant bowed down and worshipped God saying, 'Blessed be the LORD God of my master Abraham, who hath not left destitute my master of his mercy and his truth: I being in the way, the LORD led me, . . . ' [Gen. 24:27, KJV].

"When God finds you faithful," she explained, underlining her words with a measured voice, "He will lead you. Your responsibility is only to be 'in the way.' That means, you stay right where He wants you, and He'll take care of the rest. There's no safer place on earth." Hers was a lesson I shall never forget.

Later, however, it sometimes would frighten me when our children began making important choices on their own. I had a much more difficult time applying this truth to their lives than to my own. How could I be certain they were "in the way"? What if they were obviously very "out of it?" How was I supposed to trust God to lead them when they seemed so cavalier, even haphazard, about finding His will themselves? Would God require something terrible in their lives to bring them back?

Ruth Bell Graham, wife of evangelist Billy Graham, laid her heart down next to mine one day as she struggled with the same issue:

I think it harder Lord,
to cast the cares of those I love on You, than to cast mine.

We, growing older,
learn at last that You are merciful and kind.

Not one time have You failed me, Lord—
why fear that you'll fail mine?[4]

In every way that parents prize the uniqueness of each child, they will discover that God deals uniquely with each child, also. He never makes us all dance to the same tune. All of His workings are worth waiting for, but while we are waiting, there is one thing every wise parent will begin to do.

Make the Nest Less Comfortable

When a mother eagle is attempting to teach her young eaglets to fly, she often has the same problem parents do: they stand a long time teetering on the edge of the nest, deciding when they will jump, and then go back and watch television.

Mother eagles have only so much patience with this, so they have developed some clever strategies we might well pay attention to: they begin pulling the soft, fuzzy feathers out of the nest. Next, they make the couch a little less comfortable, the meals a little less appetizing, and their help a little less available. If junior wants a fresh fish, he can learn to catch it himself. Fish don't grow on trees, you know!

Likewise, we can pull out a few feathers ourselves. Remember the day I resigned? That was the day Steve and I began pulling feathers out of our nest. It was far easier than we first imagined. Allowing our nearly adult children the "privilege" of acting a little more independently actually set Steve and me free to enjoy each other more. We made plans to go out to dinner or a movie without checking everyone else's schedule first. Even a weekend away wasn't impossible. Yes, it's important to have the home front covered when you need to leave young teens, but by the time they are seventeen or eighteen, they should know the rules without another adult there to "keep watch." We started rehearsing for the empty nest days that lay ahead, something I had once dreaded that now looked a bit more inviting day by day.

I was now free to make writing a higher priority than before, and my teenagers learned to respect Mom's schedule, too. The times we were able to share together were less stressful; somehow our kids felt more on equal ground, less scrutinized, and more responsible for themselves. The outcome of our feather removal was a more relaxed nest and a more adult relationship with our kids.

Fledgling Time

As parents we need to consider whether our own efforts to be kind, generous, and accommodating might be hindering our young adults from venturing out on their own. It would be hard to leave your own free mini-apartment with private bath, laundry and meal service, fully-stocked refrigerator, pool and Jacuzzi. Now that's what I call a well-feathered nest! Sadly, I know lower income families whose parents have knocked themselves out with two and three jobs to provide an unreasonable comfort level for their teenagers. Frankly, that was a waste of money. Excessive comforts never build character and may even weaken it. It's time to start pulling feathers, folks.

When the moment finally arrives for your late-bloomer to bloom, watch out! It may happen fast, and all those days you worried and wondered will only be a memory at best. When the final push out of the nest comes, I can almost guarantee it will be a providential push you could never have thought of on your own. But Someone else was working on it all the time.

Just Thinking

Sit down with your young adult and help him or her make a list of his strengths. Take a moment to thank God for them and talk about career goals that fit his natural bent.

Next, help him address areas of weakness. Are there some that still cause hurt and hindrance? Help him find ways to manage those areas, being open about the ways you have learned to handle weakness, too. Look for increasing opportunities to highlight your child's talents in front of others.

As a couple, ask yourselves if there are ways you might begin making the nest less comfortable. Mothers may need help withdrawing from their "urge to nurture."

≥a·

CHAPTER FOUR

Rx for survival: ten skills to keep you close

*T*hey sat around the table like zombies.

"Why are these girls so quiet? They act like they aren't having any fun!" Steve whispered to me under his breath. We continued flipping pancakes on two grills simultaneously. I knew they had probably stayed up half the night giggling and talking about boys, but I wondered, too, why a room full of thirteen-year-olds could be so dull this late on a Saturday morning. Oh well, I figured, they were all in a bad mood at the same time.

"I've got a great idea," Steve snickered to himself. "Let's just see if they're really awake or not!" With that, he strode into the adjoining family room, flicked on some loud music, and yelled, "Hey, girls! Watch this!"

They looked up from their pancakes in disbelief. Steve had taken a running jump and leaped over the couch that had been moved to one end of the room between the family room and the kitchen. In midair he discovered what the girls already knew: they had also moved the coffee table to the other side of the couch. Lauren looked up in amazement as she saw her father's facial expression change the moment he realized his miscalculation.

When Steve managed to land safely in front of the coffee table, the whole room full of girls burst into applause and shrieks of praise. Lauren, at thirteen, was immensely impressed. It was a moment we recorded in the Kidder family history and still recount a dozen or so years later. After that, the laughter never stopped until the girls' parents came to pick them up. As a few cars left the driveway, I overheard, "Mom, you'll never believe what Mr. Kidder did!"

Top Ten Skills

There's nothing like making memories. Would you like to create an atmosphere in your home that makes kids want to be together as a family night after night, that keeps you close to one another, drawing a circle of safety and rest around your home? With a few simple skills, parents can create an atmosphere that reduces emotional distance and promotes healthy, loving relationships in the home. You can certainly add to this list, but here are our top ten skills to keep you close as a family.

1. Laughter and the Oil of Gladness

Howard Hendricks, who captures my attention instantly with his candid approach to life, has enriched our family immeasurably through his speaking and writing. When asked on a radio show what he thought God might say to him when he arrived in heaven, he answered, "I think He'd ask me why I didn't have more fun!" Better yet, why not ask ourselves now?

Have you ever forgotten how to have fun? Barbara Johnson in her book, *Fresh Elastic for Stretched Out Moms,* kept me laughing one summer when I thought I had forgotten how. It's so easy to take yourself and life too seriously, especially when your children are having problems. Barbara has a fresh way of looking at things:

> You can cultivate the garden of your mind and watch your days bloom one by one. . . .Underfed plants droop. So do people. Are you drooping today, arms down and spirit drooping? Check what you are being fed in your mind and your spirit. Maybe some weeding is necessary right now, some cultivation, digging out some roots of weeds that are stopping fresh growth . . . .We do believe in mixing fun with our recipe for life. He who laughs, lasts! So put guffaws, snickers, giggles, and titters high on your priority list. Sincere laughter is a powerful tonic for weary, battered souls.[1]

Weeds grow in family life, too. We clean them out by evaluating what matters and what doesn't, by centering on wholesome thoughts about one another and life rather than critical, negative and complaining thoughts, and by sowing seeds of love and affirmation in their place. Laughter softens the ground so we can dig holes to plant those seeds.

2. Taking Verbal Pictures

Another way to soften our children's hearts and sweeten the atmosphere at home is to remind them often of moments in their lives when they were particularly precious to us. Put them on center stage, making certain you include other family members and even those outside the family in your "audience." A young person's self-image just zooms at moments like these. It's like taking a verbal picture that frames his uniqueness for everyone listening. Stored like gold bullion in his memory bank, there are few things in life more valuable than parents' sincere compliments. (A word of caution: Verbal pictures should always compliment, never poke fun, or a great deal of damage could result rather than affirmation.)

Rehearse moments of tremendous courage, like the time Lauren got up from a nasty fall during an ice skating show and continued the program with a smile. Tell them how much you loved their thoughtfulness, like the way Amy always insisted on making little gifts for each brother and sister when visiting with Grammy. Do you still cherish the little wood and ceramic gifts your children made for you over the years? I love to show guests the handsome table Bob made or David's sculpture of his own hands. Do you have a son or daughter who excels at sports? Did he win a game for his team or handle loss with dignity? Capture those moments when your children were at their best in clear, enthusiastic verbal pictures. Let them know from time to time the pride you felt at their best efforts.

Our boys both won first prize in their first cross-country race at ages seven and eight on their dad's birthday. Those plaques mean the world to my husband. He will never forget that Saturday as they pumped across the finish line. He took a picture of it in his memory bank and gave it to them at different times over the years when they needed to know they could still be winners again.

Amy always had a tender heart for babies and small children. Gifted with a kind and helpful nature, she often had her "picture taken" in the family helping others.

Lauren was the counselor and confidant for anyone with a problem and an evangelist among her friends at school. Some of her "prayer projects" are now in full-time ministry.

Each child's uniqueness needs to be verbally affirmed, especially as he or she is poised to leave the nest, so that he can appreciate his tremendous value in the family. We knew times would come, and they did, when our children's personal worth and the love we had poured into their lives would be attacked, hatefully targeted by the forces in a sinful, fallen world. Publicly framing their "specialness" in a gallery of verbal pictures is one strong line of defense.

3. Living an Upbeat Faith

Steve and I recently attended a church far from home while on a weekend trip to visit my daughter and her husband. I sat quietly enjoying the beautiful atmosphere for worship, when along came a little blonde girl about eight or nine with her father. As she moved slowly into the pew in front of me, her father gave her an impatient shove with the end of his big leather Bible. I watched with horror as the little girl sat and wept quietly, head down, nursing a wounded spirit. I thought to myself, *Is she going to grow up thinking that God pushes us around with His Word, too? Will she picture Him as a bully like her dad?* I sat and prayed for that child throughout the rest of the service, resisting the temptation to give her father a big push with my hymnal when I stood behind him.

"Sour Christianity," said John Wesley, "is the devil's religion!" If there is an easier way to turn our children off to a life-walk with Jesus Christ, I don't know it. Parents who are thoroughly delighted with God's world and the work He has given them to do will do more to win their children to Christ than a hundred sermons or youth rallies.

Award-winning singer and songwriter Twila Paris recalled for *Today's Christian Woman* some of the ways her parents demonstrated an upbeat faith:

> My parents always made us feel welcome. They were never too busy "doing God's work" to give me attention. Even as a teenager, I thought I must be the most entertaining company in the world because my folks loved to be with me—and with each of my siblings. It didn't occur to me until years later that they chose to spend time with us. Their public personas also matched their lives at home: their morning quiet time, passionate love for God, humble spirit.[2]

Now there's an example that's hard to beat. It's no wonder, even as adults with busy lives, their children make it a priority to be together as a family on a regular basis.

4. Extending a Welcome

A smile and a greeting go a long way toward closing the gaps in family life.

"Hi, honey! How'd it go today?"

"Not too great! My history test was awfully hard, but I think I passed. I had a lot of fun in gym, though. We're doing field hockey and I'm really good at it. What's for supper? Oh, how was your day, Mom?"

Simple conversations maybe, but they are ligaments that connect our lives. Extending a warm welcome to each member of the family when he or she arrives home after a long day at work or school says to them, "You are important to me. Your presence makes a difference and I care about how you feel." Coming home without a welcome is like entering a house emptied of loving concern.

Steve always greeted our children when they came downstairs in the morning, or home from a friend's house, or simply entered the room—any time after being separated from them. Serendipitous moments full of meaning can happen like that. "Hi, Dad. Hey, can we talk for a minute? I've got a problem I need help with." And the bonds of love grow stronger.

As our welcome grows, so will the family circle. Over the years, a number of other young adults have identified themselves, at least in part, as members of our family. Some even call us Mom and Dad. It's wonderful fun and a great honor to be "spiritual parents" to others besides your own children. Just think! You were chosen by these precious young people, and your own children brought them home to meet you!

If I could apply for a job in heaven one day, I'd like to be the doorkeeper because it will feel like a continual party to be royally welcoming home God's children one at a time. I'm warming up for it now, how about you?

5. Displaying a Winning Attitude

In order for our faith to be winsome, the atmosphere in our home should be positive, affirming, and cheerful whenever reasonable. The world provides us with enough bad news. Put-downs, sarcasm, grumbling, and complaining are simply not fitting in a home where we hope to prepare young believers to face life for themselves. A good attitude is better than any sermon, especially when there is real reason to complain.

ATTITUDE CHECK

"If you have any encouragement from being united with Christ, if any comfort from his love, if any fellowship with the Spirit, if any tenderness and compassion, then make my joy complete by being like-minded, having the same love, being one in spirit and purpose. Do nothing out of selfish ambition or vain conceit, but in humility consider others better than yourselves. Each of you should look not only to your own interests, but also to the interests of others. Your attitude should be the same as that of Christ Jesus: . . . Do everything without complaining or arguing, so that you may become blameless and pure, children of God without fault in a crooked and depraved generation, in which you shine like stars in the universe as you hold out the word of life."

    – Philippians 2:1–5, 14–16

It's difficult to maintain this attitude day after day, especially with children going through their own rough times. We need a fresh in-filling of Holy Spirit power each day. This implies a moldable, teachable spirit on the part of parents whose greatest desire is to influence their children to follow Christ for a lifetime.

Your children are watching you. How did you get that peace and joy? How can you come home from a job where you're being treated unfairly and not bad-mouth your boss? Why will Dad go out late at night to see that there's milk for breakfast and bring home a treat for Mom who forgot to buy it? How do kids figure out parents who will put in hours when they are tired helping them finish an overdue term paper?

6. Showing a Servant Spirit

Another component of a winsome attitude is a servant spirit. That doesn't mean waiting on people hand and foot but, rather, learning to put others' needs ahead of your own. The secret of a servant spirit is knowing Christ and allowing Him to live through you in your home, especially when it's inconvenient. That may include working on cars in the rain, or driving two hundred miles to rescue your college student with a raging fever and no one to help him, or getting up at 6:00 A.M. to fix breakfast for a budding teen Bible study that wants to meet before school.

Probably the hardest thing to give is time. Most of us lead such demanding lives that even finding the time to read this book is costly. Something else had to be put aside in order to read. (But I'm glad you did!) Investing time in helping one another is a sacrificial gift of love—one that is best given as the Lord leads and in His time. Conversely, meeting every need isn't necessarily helpful. How do you know? As Anne Ortlund once said when asked what was the best advice she could give another Christian, "I'd say, obey the next prompting of the Holy Spirit."

7. Showing Grace

When our kids are struggling to become adults, they need lots of grace. As much as we love them, these same strugglers are usually so totally involved in their own lives that they are unaware of what they put others through. During this time, you may find yourself feeling used and taken for granted, and very little outward appreciation seems to be coming your way. Have patience. As my friend Judie says, "The One who is keeping the books is still in heaven." These are times for filling up their bank accounts with grace. One day your young person will draw from the undeserved kindness you've deposited in his or her account and give it freely to someone else.

Grace restores, even when it's secondhand. A young friend of ours, once a rebel, is now married and on the mission field. His attitude toward his parents' faith changed dramatically when he witnessed their loving and forgiving spirit toward his older sister when she came home from college pregnant. He saw his sister receive sacrificial help and gentle guidance in place of condemnation. When she delivered her baby and returned to college locally, her mother provided the superb babysitting new grandmothers are best at. Restoring their daughter reached deep into their son's heart, too.

God knows when your works are intended to please Him alone. He takes every loving effort on your part and weaves it into the fabric of a hurting heart to restore strength and faith when there was weakness, confusion, and hurt. The caution, however, for us is not to be manipulative. There are no bargaining chips with God.

8. Tuning Your Voice

Yesterday, I received a request by mail for a tape of a talk I had given. I found the tape quickly, wrote a letter of response, and popped them both in an envelope, then paused a moment thinking, "Maybe I should listen to this. I wonder what it sounds like?" I plugged it in the tape player. I remembered the message, but it was the sound of it that really shook me up. Was this irritating voice mine, this chirpy childish voice that took much too long telling these interminable stories? What a rude awakening when I realized that's what I sounded like to my husband and children for more than twenty-five years! They deserve a star in their crowns for patience!

There's another problem with tapes. The ones left over in our mind from our childhood never quite get erased. We play back to our own young adults the same litany that once made us wild:

- ❖ "Don't contradict me!"
- ❖ "Stand up straight."
- ❖ "Don't speak to me in that tone of voice."
- ❖ "If you think that, you've got another think comin'."
- ❖ "I'm not going to discuss this any more."
- ❖ "Is that the best you can do?"

The list goes on and on. I'm certain every teenager in the world has a list of his parents' expressions that he hates. Like burrs under a saddle, they are constant irritations that divide families rather than draw them close.

The Book of Proverbs is rich with advice for daily living, particularly regarding the power of words. Two reminders that have helped to "tune my voice" and make it less cacophonous over the years are: "Reckless words pierce like a sword, but the tongue of the wise brings healing" (Prov. 12:18), and "A gentle answer turns away wrath, but a harsh word stirs up anger" (Prov. 15:1). Reckless, harsh words wound the soul, whereas well-timed, gentle, Spirit-led words turn away anger and bring healing. One chooses to aggravate the problem, the other promotes a solution. We need to "tune" our words daily by bringing them under the authority of God's Word. When His Word is the last word, our words will be the best words.

9. Loving by Listening

I love a statement David Augsburger made in his book *Caring Enough to Be Heard.* "Being heard," he said, "is so close to being loved that for the average person they are almost indistinguishable. . . . From birth to death, listening and being listened to is the breath of our emotional life."[3]

Because we are naturally selfish individuals, the art of listening isn't born into us. It must be intentionally developed in years of practice. If you want to be a better listener to your teenager, here are a few simple tips that will help:

Learn to control your facial expressions. Practice maintaining a calm and steady gaze in the bathroom mirror every morning. No one wants to keep talking to a person whose face registers instant disapproval or alarm.

A grown woman shared with me about the night she told her parents she had tried marijuana in college. They never flinched, even though their hearts were dying inside. "I couldn't believe it," she said. "They never got angry, never overreacted. Instead, they said they loved and respected me and hoped I would never try it again. I felt so loved and accepted at that moment, I gave up fooling with drugs for good!"

Listen without talking. Listen hard and listen long. You may not get this opportunity again to understand how your young adult really feels. Treasure it, allowing ample opportunity for them to talk. If you must say something, ask questions to clarify, not to express your opinion. There are times when no one wants advice. Being heard is all that is needed.

Listen actively. Posture expresses our interest more than we realize. Look interested, even absorbed, by leaning forward, focusing on eye contact, nodding your understanding, and giving full attention. Try not to rush to the part when you can talk. This is most difficult for people like me who have an overabundance of free advice. Listening actively demonstrates a high level of respect.

Listen empathically. Steven Covey talks extensively about listening in his book, *The 7 Habits of Highly Effective People.*

"Empathic listening," he explains, is "listening with intent to understand. I mean seeking first to understand, to really understand. . . . Empathic listening gets inside another person's frame of reference. You look out through it, you see the world the way they see the world, you understand their paradigm, you understand how they feel. . . . The essence of empathic listening is not that you agree with someone; it's that you fully, deeply, understand that person, emotionally as well as intellectually."[4]

When Barbara and her teenage daughter reached an impasse in communication, they began writing letters to one another. Written late at night, or after a prayer time, their letters peeled back a layer of raw honesty both had longed for. It was painful at times, but the truth often is. Barbara's willingness to understand her daughter's deepest struggles with her faith, as well as share her own, allowed both women to become trusted adult friends.

Respond prayerfully, carefully, and respectfully. It's a great relief when we realize it isn't our responsiblity to "fix" everything we think is wrong in our young adult's life. Far better, when we turn the resolution of these matters over to our Heavenly Father, the responsibility becomes His, and we are free to show love and respectful ways of relating to one another, even when we may disagree. This doesn't mean God won't use us in powerful ways to be strong for our children or to be their protectors when needed. It means the outcome isn't ours to control. It is His to give and ours to pray into being. A wonderful partnership with God in loving, launching, and letting go is available to every parent who seeks it.

10. Sharing Our Dreams

Someone once said, "The real test of intimacy isn't in sharing our sorrows. It's in sharing our joys, our dreams."

Sharing dreams requires a sense of safety and great trust. It is like handing a piece of valuable crystal to another for him to hold. Dreams that are shattered seldom are mended to their original state. We need to treat them delicately.

"I've decided I'm going to run a hotel one day," announced ten-year-old Bruce, eldest of six, at the dinner table. "I've been thinking about it for some time, and that's what I want to do."

No one laughed. "That's great, Bruce. We'll all come and stay at your hotel one day." A dream was born, ushered delicately to life and nurtured by those who loved him. Obstacles ignored, the dream grew and Bruce disciplined it into reality.

God puts dreams in our hearts—dreams to become someone special, or to accomplish some great task. I am convinced they are given to prepare us for God's calling, to help us focus our lives and follow His leading when we might otherwise go our own way. Dreams are like fuel. They drive us ahead when the road looks impossible and inspire us to draw on God's power.

Joseph, as the Bible records, was a famous dreamer. His father, Jacob, was skeptical, knowing that Joseph's dreams of greatness would generate jealousy and hatred among his brothers. Still, we are told, "his father kept the matter in mind" (Gen. 37:11). Had God not also given big dreams to his grandfather, Abraham? Was not his father, Isaac, the fulfillment of one of those dreams? Who was he to edit God's thoughts?

A parent's job is to be so sensitive to God that he will recognize the dream that God has given and then help pray it into being.

Twila Paris recalls her parent's influence on her dreams. "Since my parents believed in me and in what God could do through me, it never occurred to me that I couldn't follow whatever dream God placed in my heart. My parents always answered my question, 'Can I do it?' with 'Of course you can.' Because of that belief, I've been resilient."[5]

May we become "Of course you can" parents. May we teach our young people to listen to God on their own, to be ready to do His bidding, to become His "Yes, I can" children who say, "Here am I, send me."

Just Thinking

How's the "tune" in your voice? List the tapes from your past that you are playing back for your young adults. Are there any that need to be erased? How about forgiven? Why not ask your son or daughter?

Talk about these ten ways to build closeness as a family. You may want to rank them in order of importance and work on just one at a time, enlisting everyone's cooperation. Then move on to the next. What ways not listed here do you consider just as important?

ଈ

Launching

Five practical skills every young adult needs

I am told that residence hall directors across the country brace themselves for the day the freshmen arrive. A parade of station wagons, U-Hauls, vans, and sway-backed family cars pulls up to the front door of the dorm and begins unloading enough clothing, stereo, television and computer equipment to make Macy's warehouse pale in comparison.

It's not that the arriving students pack all this paraphernalia; at least a third of the boxes hold last-minute items bought by moms in overdrive—First Aid kits, sinus medicine, a vaporizer, four cans of spot remover, two economy size bottles of fabric softener to go with the forty-pound box of laundry detergent, a tabletop ironing board that will never get used, a new robe and slippers, and, of course, a spare electric blanket. Parents seldom miss a thing on the list of suggested items every incoming freshman needs—even plastic flatware and a can opener. What they often miss is what can't be packed—five skills which often spell the difference between success and prolonged frustration, or even failure, that first year or two away from home.

FIRST-YEAR ADJUSTMENTS

Dr. Barbara Schoonmaker, director of Educational Development for the Department of Residential Life and Housing at the State University of New York at Albany, spoke candidly with me about the radical adjustment that life on campus brings to the more than 2,100 freshman in her charge every year. "The biggest issues involve self-discipline: managing their time, their money, and scheduling the heavy demands of their studies. Beyond that, simply adjusting to living respectfully with others can present real problems. I find the staff is having to mediate disputes between roommates more than ever before. First-year students are often finding themselves members of campus communities which are becoming increasingly more diverse."

Within the first month of school, a wide landscape of challenges opens to our newly released young adults: how to manage the mountain of mildewing laundry, how to keep from spending several weeks' living allowance on concert tickets and eating out, how to control the inner nemesis of procrastination, how to live with a crabby, self-centered roommate, and even more important to some, how to keep your car running (if you have one) when Dad's not around. These things can undo your self-confidence in a hurry!

When kids aren't prepared for life on their own, they can take years learning what might have been learned by age eighteen. You can help your child not to be one of them. Here, then, are the top five practical skills that will help your son or daughter get a head start as an independent young adult and give you peace of mind at the same time. Don't let them leave home without them.

TOP FIVE SKILLS

Skill #1—Getting Along with Others

Susan's parents had just finished helping their daughter settle her new dorm room. Pink gingham curtains, a fluffy comforter, posters for the walls . . . it looked beautiful! Her roommate had unpacked earlier, leaving a few modest attempts at homeyness that revealed little about her. Everything she owned was very simple and nearly colorless.

"Honey, I'm sure she's very nice. You'll make friends," her mother offered quiet words of comfort.

Moments later, her roommates' parents arrived, but no roommate. They introduced themselves, sat down on their daughter's bed and appeared to be waiting for her.

"Gretchen, come on in, dear. Come and meet Susan, your new roommate," her mother said, directing her voice into the hallway. No one appeared.

Susan walked softly into the hallway and tried to smile a greeting at the unkempt, rough-complected girl who looked like she wanted to blend into the wallpaper. "Hi! I'm Susan. Come on in and see how pretty our new room looks." Gretchen still didn't respond. Instead, she walked in the room with her head bowed down, dropped onto her bed, and lit a cigarette. Susan and her parents knew it was going to be a very long year.

Susan's situation may seem extreme, but it represents the type of adjustment situation any young person might face when living with a roommate who is just plain different! Opposites often fall together in dorm rooms. Invariably, one treats the room like a dumpster, the other is meticulous. One

likes rock, the other country. One studies into the wee hours
with all the lights on, the other needs eight hours of undis-
turbed sleep. Young adults preparing to leave home will need
a battery of people skills and a large reservoir of tolerance. To
some extent, these are related to a person's natural personality,
but parents can emphasize at home the importance of respect-
ing other's space, tolerating other points of view, and showing
concern for others.

Respect others' space. In the compressed environment of a
dorm room or student apartment, space becomes crucial.
Many students come from situations where they have never
had to share a room before in their lives with a younger
brother or sister.

Teach your teenagers to pick up after themselves when
they leave a room, to confine their projects, books, clothes,
and sporting gear to their own room and to allow others
uninterrupted time for reading, thought, or rest. Stress the
importance of returning borrowed items promptly or, better
yet, not borrowing them at all.

Kati is a college senior and an RA (Resident Assistant) for
over eighty freshmen at her college. She is the first person they
run to with their problems, which generally involve roommates. Kati counsels them,

> Your room is the most personal place you have away from
> home. Students have different concepts about what being
> considerate means. When another student doesn't ask be-
> fore using your CDs or your favorite sweater, or respect
> your need for peace and quiet or privacy, you feel violated.
> It boils down to communicating what your needs are from
> the beginning, laying a few ground rules that are clearly
> understood. What does each person need in terms of study
> time, time alone, permission to have friends sleep over,
> housekeeping arrangements, loud music, etc.?

Getting along with peers at college is much easier when
kids learn respect for other's space at home.

Tolerate other points of view. Exposure to the cultural blending that occurs on a college campus is one of the richest experiences your son or daughter will have, but it can also produce tensions. Whether a roommate is from South Africa, Texas, or the Bronx, there will be differences in his or her values related to dating, money, concern for others' rights, even honesty in school. Although we never want our young people to shrink from standing up for what they believe is right, a certain level of tolerance is necessary.

Accepting people from differing backgrounds is an important first step toward making a difference in those people's lives and often leads to lifetime friendships. Parents can demonstrate this kind of acceptance in two ways: making sure their conversations are never derogatory toward people of differing backgrounds, and extending hospitality to a wide variety of people.

Our children consider themselves at least part Hispanic, Chinese, and Vietnamese (what a combination!) because of close relationships developed through years of friendship with people from those countries. One year, Allie, our teenage "daughter" from Guatemala, decorated our lives while completing a year of high school in the United States. Adjusting to the cultural differences wasn't always easy, but it taught us a lot about tolerance and understanding.

Show concern for others. It's important for teenagers to learn to care for others' needs as well as their own. It seldom comes naturally, but what a blessing a thoughtful roommate can be! We've been indebted to roommates who have cared for our kids when they've been sick at college by bringing them meals, delivering assignments for them, and even taking them to the emergency room more than once.

Roommates are often the first people to learn about our children's problems at school. Carol Kuykendall, author of *Give Them Wings,* relates the story of how a roommate saved

the life of her diabetic son, Derek, in the first few days of his
freshman year.

> On the first day of classes, Derek suffered another severe
> diabetic reaction. His roommate, Erik, finally roused him
> out of bed and assumed he was on his way to the bathroom.
> But instead, Derek, wearing only his underwear went out
> the front door and wandered around in front of the dor-
> mitory, just as all the other students were rushing off to
> class. Erik, who was beginning to catch on to the symptoms
> of Derek's reactions, found him and gave him some juice.
> Derek "came to" with a horrifying realization of what he'd
> just done. . . . The very next morning, Erik found Derek
> totally unconscious. Erik called 911, and paramedics car-
> ried Derek out of the dormitory on a stretcher. [1]

Had his roommate assumed Derek was just sleeping in, he
would have died.

How do kids learn to show concern for others? They learn
it from mothers and dads who model the same concern for
others and never miss a chance to affirm their children for
doing the right thing.

A note on personal safety: Due to a recent rash of incidents
of violent crime on college campuses, I feel compelled to add
a word or two on teaching your son or daughter to be a bit
"streetwise."

Many young people enter college with very little awareness of danger. They have come from homes where Mom and
Dad watched out for them, supervised their rides and activities to and from school and social events, or at least knew who
they were with. Leaving home often means adjusting to a city
environment rather than suburban or rural.

Teach your son or daughter the importance of walking
with a friend on campus, especially late at night. Teach them
to lock their dorm rooms and car doors, and to be careful
entering a car at night. Seminars or courses on self-defense
are available on most campuses, if desired. But above all,
exercising a little caution and common sense can make the

difference between safety and being in the wrong place at the wrong time.

Skill #2—Basic Housekeeping

When our oldest daughter entered college, she had two freshman boys offer to pay her to do their laundry. Without hesitation, Lauren refused. At home she had earned her nickname, "Laundry Lauren," by doing most of our household laundry for more than a year while I recovered from a back problem. Lauren realized how unique this knowledge was when her roommate exclaimed incredulously, "You mean you know how to use fabric softener?" I guess housekeeping is a lost art among the young.

Sons, daughters, and fathers can all be taught to read fabric care labels, learn not to throw dry cleanables to their death in the washing machine, or leave wet things to mildew in the hamper. Mothers who train their teenagers to do their own laundry will hug themselves the first time their kids come home from college with six weeks of wash and do it themselves. Think of it as an investment in their future!

Another worthy investment is teaching your young adult a few cleaning skills. Even if their own room was a disaster, our kids still helped vacuum, dust, and pick up around the house. We didn't hire outside help with the house until long after our children had left the nest and our schedules demanded it. Not only is it healthier to live in clean surroundings, it's also mentally relaxing to return to a pleasant home after a long day. Even if it takes them years to decide to be neat, our young adults can enter college no stranger to a dust mop and broom.

Skill #3—Managing Time

Procrastination is the big nemesis of young adults. High school days are generally full of built-in time constraints and deadlines. Daily classes and regular marking periods help keep students on track. In college, however, the demands of heavy course loads hit with fewer classes and more self-imposed studies and combine with opportunities galore for on-campus clubs and activities. Many young people flounder. Let's be honest, self-discipline is no fun for anybody. We can, however, teach our children the sweet taste of completing their work on time, every time, and the rewards for scheduling both work and fun.

My friend Kellie is a graduate student who has struggled hard with procrastination. Getting a grip on time management has enabled her to finish undergraduate school on time (which, incidentally, very few students do these days), complete one Master's degree, and begin a second. "Guilt," Kellie confessed, "used to tie me down. You can't have any fun when you feel guilty all the time about work that's not done. When I finally realized that, I learned to schedule time for fun. That made it easier to force myself to study when I had to."

A daily planner is a must for college students. There are many varieties on the market. Help your son or daughter learn to use a schedule book at least a year before moving out on his own. Kellie's trick of scheduling both work and play, and even planning rewards for completed tasks, is the sugar coating on the self-discipline pill.

Another helpful trick is learning to plan backwards. Teach your teenager to reserve the hours needed to complete a term paper or prepare for a test by working backward from the goal, breaking it down into a series of smaller tasks each day. That's the way I'm writing this book. Deadlines look less like henchmen and tensions are greatly reduced when work looks "doable" rather than impossible.

Skill #4—Managing Money

"I can't believe it!" the young man seethed, tossing an opened letter in disgust on his desk. "The bank says my account is overdrawn by $200! Don't they know I changed banks?"

"Well, did you leave enough money in your account to pay for all the checks you wrote?" his friend asked.

"How should I know? My dad takes care of all that stuff!"

Managing money can be a rude awakening for many college students. Living in a dormitory with regular meals and no bills isn't too big a challenge for most young people during their first year or two at college, but the problems mount quickly as dorm life gives way to a fraternity or sorority house or student apartment. With no meal plan and an active social life, money can get out of control quickly. Add to that a car on campus and you may find yourself hyperventilating when the phone rings and it's your son or daughter calling about another big bill.

Just to give you fair warning, many colleges also attach student parking tickets to the parents' monthly tuition bill, plus towing charges and fines for overdue books. Steve and I have learned to sit down before opening a bill from the bursar's office.

It's hard not to bail our children out all the time. They sound so pathetic on the phone that our natural sympathies can overrule wisdom. We have, by necessity, required each of our children to pay for part of their college education through scholarships and student loans. In addition, they all held part-time jobs for spending money. Still, summer savings were seldom enough to make it past even the first semester, and bail-outs became frequent. Had we turned earlier to experts like Larry Burkett, we might have followed his advice and trained our young adults to budget their money as well as their time.

In his book *Using Your Money Wisely*, Larry says, "There is no greater financial asset that parents can leave their children than the knowledge of how to establish and live on a balanced budget. Overspending should be so discouraged in

Christian homes that children wouldn't even consider it a possibility in their own homes later."[2]

I would add two words of caution to Larry's advice. First, if I had to choose between raising generous children and fiscally disciplined children, I would choose generous, hands down. Second, using money as a weapon to control our young adults' lives breeds resentment and emotional distance in relationships that will last far longer than tuition payments.

Skill #5—Basic Car Care

"What do you mean you lost my car? Where is it?" Terry's voice rose an octave, her eyes flashing in anger at her friend.

"I don't know," she shrugged. "I left it in the intersection, and when I came back, it was gone."

"You left my car in an intersection? Why?" Terry screamed.

"It just stopped, that's all, and all the red lights came on. I didn't know what else to do. I was late, so I just got out and left it there. Somebody must have towed it away. Sorry."

I must admit, when Terry told this story in our living room, our whole family was rolling on the floor with laughter. The day it happened, it wasn't funny at all. Terry finally reclaimed her car after the campus police charged her a hefty sum for towing. Naturally, her friend didn't have any money.

About 60 percent of college students have some form of wheels on campus. That's a lot of money in auto insurance, tires, gas, and oil changes, and a big responsibility to boot—one that's probably best postponed until after the first year at school. However, once the decision has been made, some basic car knowledge will make the experience much better. Here are a few tips:

❖ Teach your son or daughter how to check oil, water, and transmission fluids regularly, how to look for puddles under the car (green or red puddles mean "Don't drive it!"), and how to check the tires for air.

- Everyone should know how to change a tire in an emergency, or at least have a can of "instant air" in the trunk.

- Provide your son or daughter's car trunk with a set of jumper cables and teach him how to use them carefully. Remind him that, wrongly connected, batteries can explode.

- Teach him what all the warning lights mean, especially the oil and temperature gauge, making sure he knows that driving a car with the warning lights on can ruin its engine permanently.

- Provide your son or daughter with an auto club membership for emergencies such as running out of gas, needing a tow, having a dead battery, or being stuck in mud or snow.

- Make certain your son or daughter understands the limits of his insurance liability, what to do in the event of an accident, and the dangers of allowing other students to borrow his car. Police can seize a car containing drugs and are under no obligation to return it, regardless of whether or not the owner of the car was involved.

- Make it clear from the beginning that parents don't pay parking tickets. At our son's college, tickets double and triple with repeated offenses. After paying a few huge fines for parking in a reserved space when he was late for class, our son learned to arrive on time and walk a little farther. Speeding tickets are much worse. My insurance agent assures me most companies will refuse to insure a student who receives more than two tickets.

Well, there you have it—five practical skills that will help guarantee successful adjustment to living away from home. "Train a child in the way he should go," the familiar proverb teaches, "and when he is old he will not turn from it" (Prov. 22:6). Most often we think of this proverb as referring to the spiritual dimensions of a child's life, but it's equally true in the rhythms of daily living. We reap what we sow, and that begins earlier than any of us realized.

JUST THINKING

Give yourself a pat on the back for planning ahead to help your son or daughter be well prepared to leave home. Why not take inventory of more than socks and underwear? Ask yourselves as parents, "How are we doing in training our teenager in these five basic skills? What areas need more attention?"

Next, query your son or daughter about his or her own feelings of competence in each skill. What weak spots does he need help with? Recognizing you both are targeting his future independence can make this an exciting project. Have fun building for the future!

ôð

CHAPTER SIX

Seasoned parents and salty kids: how to make your kids hungry for your values

*H*ave you ever wondered, as I have, why some Christian homes, appearing so well structured and precept-perfect, don't always release strong, robust Christian kids who want to carry their values into the world? In contrast, we meet kids whose parents may have been irregular church attenders, yet they are thankful, appreciative of their parents, and bold in their willingness to follow God. What makes the difference? What makes kids want to leave home with their parents' values and faith firmly intact?

To find the answer, we have to look first into the foundation and infrastructure of the home. How was it built? Who built it, and what's it built on? Then, we peek in the windows.

"It's Hard to Find a Good Builder"

I've always loved new homes. They call my name. For years on Saturday afternoons my mother and I traipsed through every model home in the Capital District to satisfy my curiosity. I just wanted to be "ready" in case I found something a bit bigger and a bit more exciting than our home. I never did. Instead, I found a lot of stunning homes with shoddy workmanship. Having looked at enough eye beams, joists, and foundations, I've learned a little about the way houses are built. It's not surprising that Psalm 127 caught my attention in my devotions one morning, when I realized God, in fact, knows more than anybody about building. Here it is in its entirety:

> Unless the LORD builds the house,
>   its builders labor in vain.
> Unless the LORD watches over the city,
>   the watchmen stand guard in vain.
> In vain you rise up early
>   and stay up late,
> toiling for food to eat—
>   for he grants sleep to those he loves.
>
> Sons are a heritage from the LORD,
>   children a reward from Him.
> Like arrows in the hands of a warrior
>   are sons born in one's youth.
> Blessed is the man
>   whose quiver is full of them.
> They shall not be put to shame
>   when they contend with their enemies in the gate.

Why, I asked, did God mix two different issues in one psalm? Why talk about building houses and rearing children in the same breath? What did foundations, bricks, stones, and rafters have to do with the family sitting around the dinner table at night? After straining my limited mental powers over this issue, I finally asked God in prayer. I pictured His surprise.

"Virelle, don't you see the comparison here? People build houses, I build homes and families."

It had never even dawned on me that God might have been talking about the same thing: building homes and building families. It wasn't until we put an addition on our too-small house (the compromise to moving) that I could visualize the real meaning of this psalm.

One summer many years ago our family watched with sighs of wonder at the building of our new family room. First, a big yellow backhoe rolled up to dig an enormous hole in our backyard. All the kids in the neighborhood came over to have their picture taken on the backhoe. Next, a cement truck poured a precisely measured and heavily reinforced foundation where the hole had been. It looked huge—almost twice as big as we'd imagined. What a room this was going to be! We moved the kitchen table out onto the new foundation as soon as it was dry. They would have to build the room around us.

Fortunately, Uncle Dennis was our builder and a very tolerant man. He is also a master builder, accustomed to building homes in the Catskill Mountains that look like they should be featured in *Architectural Digest*. No one else could have built our room as beautifully as Dennis, not only because of his great skill, but because of his love for our family. He planned to visit and enjoy it with us. Dennis knew it would become a place of great fellowship for years.

Day by day we watched Uncle Dennis and his crew lay strong beams in place on that foundation. It seemed like magic the way he turned ordinary wood into this beautiful sanctuary where large windows frame the beauty of the outdoors.

This room also framed our children's growth into men and women. Youth groups shook the walls with laughter, love bloomed here, conversations challenged lives, and prayer changed us all. Marriage proposals happened here, kids danced with excitement in their Christmas pajamas, and one small dog named "Laidy" thought she owned it all.

Beams that Will Hold Your Weight

When Uncle Dennis had completed our family room, he said, "Come here, kids. I want to show you how strong these beams are! They hold the whole room up so that it will never fall down."

With that, he leaped straight up in the air, grabbing one of the huge cross beams in his big hands and swung himself back and forth like an acrobat. Suddenly, to our total amazement, he did a complete flip up over the beam and lifted himself up until his head touched the ceiling.

"See, kids," he called down to four adoring faces, "if it holds my weight, it's bound to hold yours. Who's next?" One by one Dennis lifted the children onto the beam, letting them hang on bravely for a few seconds, full of happy squeals and legs flying in all directions. It was a moment we all recall fondly, and it carries a truth that speaks even now.

God is the Master Builder who lays an unshakable foundation in the Person of His Son and builds us like living stones into a home and family for Himself. God also plans to live in the families He is building. His Word tells us clearly, "In him you too are being built together to become a dwelling in which God lives by his Spirit" (Eph. 2:22). He sets strong beams in place that will bear His name throughout the generations and build the kind of strength and character that will hold all the weight we could possibly place on them: beams called faith, love, goodness, knowledge, perseverance, godliness, self-control, kindness, patience, and obedience. They are the values we pass on to our children—the infrastructure of the Christian home. Without them our homes can break apart under pressure.

How can parents ensure that their children will grasp their values firmly and carry them into their adult lives? First, we have to make those values like popcorn at the movies—irresistible.

THREE WAYS TO SALT YOUR HOME

I love salty food. I'll choose it over dessert every time. Popcorn, salted nuts, pretzels, tortilla chips, Mexican food, pizza, you name it! If it's salty, I probably love it (with the exception of anchovies and sardines). Salty food also creates a thirst that drives me to the refrigerator again and again for something to drink. A small price to pay.

Causing our young adults to want our values is a little like feeding them salty food. We want to make them thirsty for what we have. The salt we offer is the honest demonstration of those values at home.

"Let your conversation be always full of grace, seasoned with salt," Paul reminds us (Col. 4:6). Salt preserves goodness, adding flavor and interest to the otherwise commonplace elements of life. Salty parents who are full of grace and acceptance toward one another and their children create a thirst in their children for the things of God. They accomplish this in the simplest areas of everyday life.

1. Show Them You're Real

William J. Bennett, former Secretary of Education and author of the best-selling *The Book of Virtues,* strikes the same chord. "It has been said that there is nothing more influential, more determinant, in a child's life than the moral power of quiet example. For children to take morality seriously they must be in the presence of adults who take morality seriously. And with their own eyes they must see adults take morality seriously."[1]

It's commonly felt that faith and values are more caught than taught, but I believe they are both caught and taught. In the early years, when children ask disarmingly honest questions about life, they need a lot of explaining. Children of all ages deserve honest answers every time without any deceit. But by the time they are teens, their experiences in the "real world" have so shaken their faith and values that parents need to prove them again in everyday life experiences. During this time, your teenagers are watching to see if you live the way you taught. Are you for real? Or were those explanations you gave over the years only platitudes, the "right things to say"?

By the time your children are teens or young adults, there's little left you are going to teach them. They've heard you and everyone else say it all many times. This is the time for faithful demonstration of everything you've taught. Here are a few important ways to do that:

Have you taught responsibility? Then deliver on everything you said you would do. If you offered the car, promised a pizza party, or committed yourself to attend a concert or game, make certain you do it regardless of how inconvenient it may become. I remember driving Amy to youth group even though Steve was in the hospital, and I have known parents whose faithfulness has far outdone our own. Parents who deliver on their promises are representing a Heavenly Father who delivers, too.

Have you held a high standard for honesty and truthfulness? Apply the same standard to yourself. Be scrupulously careful about every word and leave nothing unsaid that should be said. Don't leave yourself a way out of sticky situations lest you find yourself a hypocrite in your teenager's eyes. Did you spend too much money at a sale, get a speeding ticket, or dent the car? Do you ever say, "Tell them I'm not home," when the call is one you'd rather not take? Humble pie is easier to eat now than the stale bread of regret later.

Has your choice of entertainment been a reflection of your moral values? Do you view magazines, movies, and television shows that are questionable? Unchecked, all forms of pornography are very destructive. We had a policy of previewing even PG-13 movies before allowing our teens to watch them. I am amazed to learn how many Christian parents watch R-rated movies themselves and allow even young children to do the same. How can we do that and expect our children to believe God's moral standards are true?

Do you like to be spoken to with kindness and respect? Be the first to show it yourself. If you are a Christian then grace and mercy are yours. Give them to your child as freely as you receive them. When a teen or young adult is at odds with the family and his or her whole world, we want to hurt him for the ways he is hurting us, but it does no good, "for man's anger does not bring about the righteous life that God desires" (James 1:20). Far better to stop, think grace first, then act.

What makes teens hungry for their parents' values during these critical years of loving, launching, and letting go? Their appetite for the Truth will be whet only by parents who are real and never fake, who show their children what they've been telling them all these years, because there's never been a time when our children have needed so badly to see the Truth fleshed out.

2. Focus on Character, Not Performance

Imagine yourself ten or twenty years from now reflecting on these demanding days in your life as a parent. What would be important to you? Would you care so much if someone moved your tools, left the milk out, wore her hair in an awful style, or, worse yet, your son wore (gasp!) an earring?

Our three youngest were all teenagers at the same time. We had marvelous fun together but we also had times of ridiculous stress over pointless issues. I remember coming unglued over clothes that weren't put in the dryer on time, or lacrosse sticks in the front hall, or sneakers worn to church. Those things seemed monumental at the time, but if they had been allowed to become controlling issues, they could have destroyed our last opportunities to show our teens how much we loved them and how much God loves them.

HOW IMPORTANT IS IT ANYWAY?

Steve and I concluded that we should spend our last efforts with our children focusing more on character than performance. Did our sixteen-year-old have a messy room? Close the door. Was one of the children not performing up to his abilities at school even after prodding, outside help, and fair consequences for poor grades? Give him full responsibility for his own plans after high school, recognizing the limited options he will have as a result. Are you fussing every day over eating habits, hair styles, and clothing? Weigh the seriousness and then decide if you still need to make an issue of it. You may need to lose a few checkers, as Howard Hendricks once said, to win the game.

Where issues affected lifelong character, our children knew Steve and I considered them "unbendables." We had spent years lifting a high standard for honesty, courtesy, and respect at home, and kindness to everyone. Nothing had changed. Talking back, using nasty language to one another, or even saying "Shut up!" were never tolerated. I wince when I hear adults talk disrespectfully to their children or to each other. What seeds of anger are planted with each word. How much better to sow love.

3. Be Available

One of the most effective ways to salt the home and make kids hungry for your values is to be regularly and dependably available to them. Make the time to share yourself with your children. It is seldom convenient and it is never optional.

When our son, David, graduated from high school and prepared to leave home for college, his oldest sister, Lauren, gave him a copy of *Honest to God* by Bill Hybels, pastor of the Willow Creek Community Church in South Barrington, Illinois. It challenged Dave to consider the ways his faith would meet nose to nose with the tougher issues of life.

Bill Hybels pastors one of the largest and fastest growing congregations in America. A former chaplain for the Chicago Bears, he has authored many books and "shepherded" countless fledgling seeker-sensitive churches into being. I was interested to know how he "got that way." What made the difference in Bill Hybels' life that caused him to want nothing less than God's best? Not surprisingly, it was his father. Bill relates a story about him that tells volumes:

> As my brother and I approached junior high school, our dad became concerned that we would find the church youth group boring and lose interest in spiritual concerns. So he bought an old Greyhound bus, tore the seats out, and installed a small kitchen and some bunk beds. With two other fathers, he took the boys in the youth group on trips to places like Niagara Falls, Mackinac Island, and Mammoth Cave. None of the men could cook, so the food was terrible. And none knew how to teach Bible studies, so our formal training was nonexistent. But what memories!
>
> I knew, even as a little guy, that Dad was busy and had many people tugging at his time. I knew he could have been doing deals instead of driving a Greyhound bus around the Midwest with ten rebellious junior high boys. But he was determined to transform what could have been a discouraging era in our spiritual formation into an adventure. He knew his goal: to produce difference makers, spiritual champions, children who could grow up to be impact players for the cause of Christ.
>
> My dad was an eccentric man who did unconventional things to keep us kids from straying off the path. Some people even thought he went overboard. But from his vantage point in Heaven, I bet he's eternally glad he did![2]

You and I may not be inclined to buy an old Greyhound bus, but we can still put in our time in other ways. Steve spent countless hours refurbishing a 1969 Firebird convertible with our teens. Precious to our kids are memories of evening prayers in the bunk house at our primitive wilderness camp in the Adirondack Mountains, then telling stories until we fell asleep watching the fading glow of the kerosene heater.

I know of parents who helped their teens grow prize-winning gardens for the county fair, taught them to ride horses and compete in shows, learned to ride a unicycle and taught it at summer workshops, read and discussed classic literature, played chess, spent hours exploring a trout stream, or an entire afternoon riding the "Cyclone" roller coaster longer than anyone's ever done before. It can be done.

Ann Landers' column caught my eye one morning as I was sipping coffee and preparing to write this book. A woman from Illinois wrote about the reasons she hungered for her parents' faith and values. Her letter is worth sharing.

> Dear Ann Landers: I read an article recently in the *St. Louis Post-Dispatch* about teaching values to our children. The writer said, "If there is a simple way to instill in children the qualities that will keep them happy and help them contribute to the world while doing no harm to others, I have not found it."
>
> Well, I have found it—by imitating my father. He taught me by example. He went to work every day and was home to have dinner with us in the evening. He had a strong faith in God. If he could help someone in need, he did. He was always considerate of his parents and treated my mother with respect.
>
> My dad grew up in the Depression and went to work to help support the family before finishing eighth grade. He was a side gunner in World War II. Once, while visiting my grandmother in the nursing home, he found a $5 bill on the sidewalk and turned it in at the office.

My father taught me honesty, respect, courage, faith, responsibility and kindness. I thank God every day for giving me such a fine role model. I am happily married to a man who is very much like my dad. We will celebrate our 15th anniversary next month. We have four children. I hope I can instill the virtues in my children that my dad taught me.—Peggy in O'Fallon, Ill. [3]

No doubt some of you reading this could have written similar letters about both of your parents. If so, you are blessed. Even more important, wouldn't it be wonderful if our own young adults found such a compelling model in us?

God is in the business of building strong homes and families where He is pleased to live. As parents, may we be true to Him by living the values that honor His name, by loving our young adults through their highs and lows, and remaining His salty children, too.

JUST THINKING

How solid are the beams in your home? Are there some which will support weight and others that will not? How about neatness, high academic standards, manner of dress? All these values have some merit, but are they adequate as a foundation for life? As a family, talk about the values that really matter to God. Pray together as to which should be the top two or three and begin to aim at them in the remaining days before your children leave home.

As parents, does God find your conversation "full of grace and seasoned with salt"? In what ways could your example become even more authentic and winsome?

ঌ

CHAPTER SEVEN

Learning to steer in God's direction: eight major potholes to avoid

*I*t was a wet night in early spring, not a pretty time in the northeast. Leftover snowdrifts lined the roadside, winter's icy fingers refusing to let go. "Pneumonia weather" my mother calls it: temperatures teasingly warm during the day and biting cold at night. The sap is running and so is everything else, a dripping world of runoff that bodes both promise and risk for many things—not the least of which is driving—every road an obstacle course of bottomless potholes that threatens to undo your nerves and your car's suspension. It was into this scene that our family piled into our car one March night after the big middle school spring concert and headed merrily for the ice cream shop to celebrate a job well done.

"Look out, Dad!" one of the kids warned, as we pulled into the parking lot, pointing to the large, vacuous black hole in our path. "There's a huge hole in front of us!"

"What hole?" said Steve with an air of fatherly certainty. "There isn't any hole. I can't see anything!"

"Steve, stop the car!!" I shrieked, joined now by a chorus of voices screaming the same refrain.

"But I can't see any—" Too late. His next breath was a gasp as the entire right front end of our station wagon dropped crippled onto its frame into the hole, tire blown, irrevocably sunk in the cold, cavernous mush.

It was so ludicrous there was nothing to do but laugh. As Steve surveyed the damage, we rolled with laughter from inside the car, rehearsing what would echo down the next decade as our famous "Look out, Dad!" story. Poor Steve! How he wished he'd listened.

Parenting, especially the releasing end, has significant potholes, too. We might have avoided getting hung up on a few ourselves had someone warned us beforehand. In this chapter I will be riding in your front seat pointing to the big ones and yelling "Look out!" It may not be too late to swing things around and make a few timely corrections to your course.

The last leg of parenting isn't the best time to correct mistakes, but then, is anything ever too hard for you and God to accomplish together? We can at least do our best to follow the directives in His Word that help us steer in the right direction.

If one of these errors rubs you the wrong way, mark it and come back. God may be tapping you on the shoulder to straighten your course before it's too late. He's tapped us lots of times. Here, then, are the more common places to trip up in releasing your teen to adulthood.

POTHOLE 1—POWER-HUNGRY PARENTS

"Where's Dan? Has anybody seen Dan yet?" the music director called out as he gave the last two heavy amplifiers a shove into the van. The new sound system had been purchased by the kids themselves from summer-long team work: car washes, "rent-a-slave" day, a truckload fruit sale, you name it. Everyone had poured his heart into one dream—financing the first holiday concert tour of "His Image" singers.

It had begun as Dan's dream, really, after a retreat sing-a-long had sounded almost professional. He organized weekly practices and coerced a talented young music teacher who had once sung with "The Internationals" into helping them. Now where was he? They had to be in Pittsburgh by six and that was four hours away.

"Someone go call his home and see if he's left yet," one of the others kids yelled, adding, "cause I ain't singin' no solo without him as backup!"

A few minutes later, one of the girls in the group burst out of the church door into the parking lot, noticeably in tears. "Dan's not coming! His dad won't let him! He said something about a big fight last night 'cause he got home a little late. What are we going to do?"

"I can't believe this? How could his dad do this to Dan, or to us, for that matter? Doesn't he realize how hard we've worked . . . Dan's worked . . . for this tour? I'm sure he'll listen to me if I talk to him," the music director ran quickly indoors to the phone, returning only moments later, his face dark and quiet. Everyone knew it had happened again. Dan's dad never changed his mind, right or wrong, and he never thought he was wrong.

Have you known parents like this, or kids who have to live with them? Most of us are guilty of unreasonableness at times, but a parent who always has to punish, has to have the last word, and is given to harsh punishments even of older teen-agers is a parent who is about to lose the whole ball game. They are more devoted to maintaining a sense of power and control than really loving their young adult.

Would you like to know what happened to Dan after this major disappointment? When he left home the following year for college, he never returned. He had the last word. Kids usually do. Dan will probably be all right, but his mother and dad will suffer the loss of a relationship that could have been among the most precious and richest they'd ever known.

Gary Smalley talks about this type of parent in his book *The Key to Your Child's Heart:*

> The dominant parent . . . tends to produce the most negative qualities in children. Dominant parents usually have very high standards and expectations. But they seldom offer warm, caring support and very few explanations are given for their rigid rules. They tend to be unbending and demand that their children stay away from certain activities because of their strong convictions. [1]

Unfortunately, many otherwise wonderful Christians are power-hungry parents who leave a legacy of weakness, hurt, and low self-esteem in their children. Their love just doesn't reflect the same kind of love God has for His children. Of course, God knows what's best for us and He often uses difficult circumstances to teach us to listen to Him and depend upon His guidance. But His disciplines are designed to build up, not break down—to create Christlikeness, not anger. Dan's parents could have clipped his wings in another way, or, better yet, shown grace and respect to him by reminding him politely that they'd appreciate a call next time he was going to be late. How much better to gain the young person than win such a small battle.

POTHOLE 2—FLIMSY FAMILY FUN

"Steamroller!" our son-in-law Michael yelled from the family room floor where all four of our young adults and their assorted friends, buddies, and future mates were lined up like sardines in a can watching a funny movie in the dark. With that, Michael rolled his football player-sized frame across the floor full of laughing, screaming bodies. Soon, it became a war cry.

"Steamroller!" came another voice and then squeals and bedlam for about two or three minutes. Michael has certainly added a lot to our family.

We've known lots of teenagers and college students over the years who didn't want to go home. Why not? A dull, quiet household where no one laughs, holds interesting conversations, or entertains friends isn't much fun. More commonly these days is the decision where to go to "find" home—Dad's apartment or Mom's house, which sometimes include the newest girlfriend or male companion. Even worse, home has become a place where no one's home and the meals are the latest microwave main dish.

If your home isn't the happiest, most fun place your kids could be, there's something wrong. You need someone like Michael to liven things up. Love and intimacy in a family are created in many shared life experiences, not the least of which is fun. Fun is the sparkle in a home that makes our children and their friends want to keep coming back. It closes the emotional distance that builds up like plaque on our busy lives. The reason many families have fallen into the pothole of flimsy family fun is that it takes time, planning, commitment, and cleanup. It doesn't just happen.

Bill Sanders in his book *Almost Everything Teens Want Parents to Know* talks about the cost involved: "Amazingly, the reason for some of the greatest successes in families, as well as in life, may lie in the little things. Spending time together, enjoying each other doesn't look so little when you realize it takes time. Today's one- and two-parent families don't have much, if any, spare time, but this precious commodity means the most to young people as they grow up."[2]

As fun as our home has been over the years, I don't think we even approach the home Michael came from. His parents went to such great lengths as to practically choreograph memories. With seven children, that meant someone had to do a lot of planning when it would have been easier instead to turn on the television.

Let me give you just one example. Every Thanksgiving, Michael's family plays touch football on the lawn while the turkey is cooking. A few years ago, they had team jerseys printed in two colors for the whole burgeoning bunch. Next they printed a hilarious program with the weekend's schedule of food and fun, including hiking, movies, meals, and surprises. Everyone was free to join in or sneak away for a nap. It's not uncommon for single-parent families to "attach" themselves to the McGarry household at times like these. No matter which team you're on, it's a winning example.

POTHOLE 3—MAINLY MANIPULATION

"I don't know how I'll manage when you're gone next year. Couldn't you have chosen a college around here? There are so many good ones. Bobby Cushman really likes the community college. Maybe if we bought you a new car instead of spending all that money on tuition . . . "

Sound familiar? Let me introduce you to Ima Whiner, Empress of Manipulation. She's married to the King of Sarcasm who keeps his family nervous and unsure of themselves through fear, criticism, and ridicule. People just "love" spending time with them. The truth is their children are dying to get away from home but are doomed to a life of carefully planted parental guilt when they do.

Jan Silvious in her book *Please Don't Say You Need Me* deals with this issue beautifully:

> Parents who choose this form of control often are emotionally needy themselves and are merely following a pattern learned from their own childhood. If they have failed to experience unconditional love and acceptance, if their self-esteem is flagging, if they are insecure, then they may wrongly look to their children to fulfill their needs.

Manipulation is often softer than sarcasm and more winsome than put-downs. It can take the form of hurt feelings, tears, comments such as, "You really should have" and "If you cared, you would have." Frequent bouts of feeling bad and even chronic lateness can be very artful in controlling conscientious adult children. [3]

If in any way this describes you, run, don't walk, to the nearest Christian bookstore and buy Jan's book. It is a marvelous resource and offers real biblical advice for reversing the damage already done and finding healing in your own life, too. If you want the book even faster, send your young adult son or daughter to the bookstore for you.

Really letting go means allowing our young adults to make their own decisions and supporting them when they are within the realm of possibility, and sometimes when they're not. It means backing off from expecting your child to meet your emotional needs; it means substituting prayer for complaining and praise for criticism. It means accepting the challenge to become a mentor for your child rather than a manipulator by allowing God to create a real faith-life in you. It means allowing God to change you before He changes anyone else. It will be both the hardest and the best thing you have ever done.

POTHOLE 4—WORDS THAT WOUND

Sarcasm, put-downs, and ridicule are all feathers on the same vulture. The exception is, this bird doesn't wait until its victims are dead. It devours them alive, one biting word at a time.

Oswald Chambers, whose words often leave me amazed and speechless (which is really saying something!), once pointed out, "Sarcasm is the weapon of the weak man (or woman); the word literally means to tear flesh from the bone."[4] Words are the most dangerous weapons we can use on another human being because they never cease wounding. They continue tearing people apart for a lifetime.

Sarcastic people often think they are funny. I know I did, that is until I realized the pain it caused others. Some use words to gain control over others, holding them fearful and subdued lest they set themselves up for attack. There is seldom a "safety zone" in the target range of a sarcastic parent. Every area of a soft spirit is vulnerable, exposed.

Jesus' words in Matthew 12:36–37 helped me see my particular need to control a runaway sense of humor: "But I tell you that men will have to give account on the day of judgment for every careless word they have spoken. For by your words you will be acquitted, and by your words you will be condemned." Now that's laying it on the line! I hope I'm not the only one who feels uncomfortable with these verses.

If our words can wound, they can also be trained to heal under the Lord's control. If they can tear down, they can also build. Will you join me in praying daily for Christ's control of our words that they might heal and build along with Him?

POTHOLE 5—DISPLAYED DISHONESTY

* "Hey, don't worry, son. I know somebody on the police force who'll take care of that ticket for you. He does it for me all the time."

* "I haven't got time to talk to Mrs. Bamberg right now. Tell her I'm in the shower."

* "You might want to pray for Ron and Janet. Confidentially, I heard they might lose their house they're so deeply in debt. I can't believe how much Janet buys. She's always showing up in some new outfit."

* "There's no way I'm going to apologize to my sister. She's the one who always starts it. Let her come to me first. I'm not wrong this time!"

One of the most subtle potholes any of us can fall into is the pothole of displayed dishonesty. Caught off-guard, our words reveal what's really inside—pride, lust, gossip, trickery, bad language, you name it. It's like turning over a rock to see a host of ugly little sins we've pushed aside. The problem is that our children are looking under our rock all the time and remembering what they've seen and heard. Likewise, when our conversation with one another is predominantly arguing and complaining at home, our faith is a lot less believable. Our example speaks louder than the hundreds of hours of instruction we've invested in their preparation for adulthood.

MAKING THINGS RIGHT

What can you do to undo the damage when you've been caught with your proverbial "pants down"? Admit it. Make it right—first with God and next with your son or daughter. Any other way out is a dead end. Your willingness to admit failure, to own up to your blunder, will communicate far better than anything else what Christianity is all about.

The fact is we are really hopelessly sinful people who would be doomed to an eternal hell without the saving blood of Jesus Christ—an extravagant gift lovingly poured out on our behalf on the cross. Tell your young adult that. Tell them you will never outgrow your need for daily forgiveness. You haven't got the corner on perfection, and you need their forgiveness, too. It's very level ground at the foot of the cross—a place where we often meet our adult children for the first time as equals.

POTHOLE 6—LACKLUSTER LOVE

One of the most easily rationalized potholes parents fall into is the sinkhole of lackluster love. It could also be called "lazy love" because it describes the parent who's given up trying to be loving to his or her spouse. The zing has fizzled. The last thing their kids will ever find Dad doing is fooling around with Mom in the kitchen. And why would he want to? She gave up behaving like his girlfriend years ago.

"She knows I love her. I come home on time every night, don't I? I bought her a new car last year. Isn't that enough?"

"He would rather sit in that recliner channel-surfing than talk to me about my day or what I think. I just can't get his attention. I guess we're getting too old for romance anyway."

Baloney! If you can still remember why you fell in love with each other, it's not too late to rekindle the lovelife you long for with your mate and restore your young adult's faith in God's plan for marriage and commitment at the same time. By the time teens are readying themselves for departure, husbands and wives should be turning their attentions firmly to one another as a top priority. It's not selfish as some may argue, but an investment in the rest of your lives that will reap interest for generations.

You see, true love is winsome, sacrificial, extravagant, and contagious. It is always truthful, never dividing loyalties by saying things like, "Don't let your father know about this. We'll just keep this little matter to ourselves, OK?" Rather, it builds up respect for its mate in the eyes of the children: "Dad is so amazing the way he handles all the conflict at work and never comes home grouchy." Or, "Mom will know just the right thing to say to your friend. She always does."

This kind of love is the embodiment of the whole of Scripture, a living illustration of the passionate love of God for His Bride, the Church. Make your marriage all it can be by asking God to turn you into the kind of man or woman your mate would want to marry all over again.

How can a single parent accomplish this? By never bad-mouthing marriage and by regularly pointing out Christian couples who are thoroughly in love with one another. Look for every opportunity for your teen to spend time with them.

POTHOLE 7—THE "THINGS TRAP"

I was driving to our high school one brilliant autumn afternoon to pick up assignments for a student I was tutoring, when a flash of red raced past my car and nearly ran me off the road. As it passed me, I observed an impatient young man in a new BMW convertible, one arm draped casually over the wheel, the other hand cradling a car phone. Seething, I followed him to his destination and was incredulous to find it was the same as mine! The high school! He hopped out, book bag in hand, and ran to class! I promptly went inside and reported him for reckless driving.

How does it happen that the student cars in the school parking lot are often nicer than the faculty cars? I asked my kids this same question and they looked at me amazed at my naïveté. "Mom, their parents buy them those cars. Most of the kids have nice cars these days. Incidentally, I wouldn't mind having one myself. "

"Neither would I," I answered with raised eyebrow.

Materialism is a two-pronged fork. On the one hand, it pierces our pocketbook, making it leak unbearably every payday, and on the other hand, it pierces our soul by watering down our interest in the bigger issues of life. The "things trap" sinks families into the habitual bondage of wanting more all the time and reduces the idea of contentment to a Sunday School platitude. For many, the coveted objects that once promised pleasure have instead tightened the handcuffs of debt, and the fun and freedom we dreamed would be ours turned out to be an illusion.

One older woman recently confided another type of fall-out to me. "When I was growing up, my mother would never let us have parties or even just have friends over because she was always so worried about the house. It had to be perfect. We could never use our good glasses for our friends or even our family because they might get broken. Things were never nice enough for her, and yet they were too good to use for our friends. I grew up resenting her for that."

If you find yourself in the "things trap" in any way at all, there is one sure way to get free: Give everything you own back to God! Ask Him how to use it, where to spend it, and on whom. Let Him pour out a blessing on your life by making yours a home breeding givers rather than getters. How much more like your Heavenly Father you will become!

POTHOLE 8—THE PERFECT PARENT

You've probably figured out by now that I'm not a perfection-ist. My husband Steve is, however, and probably wishes I were a lot more like him. Actually, I do, too. When Steve cleans up the kitchen it looks like Grandma Kidder were alive again. When he edits my writing, I brace myself, knowing it's going to come back looking like a Christmas tree.

Steve is a controlled perfectionist, meaning that he's still messy enough to be fun to live with. But when it comes to parenting, we both suffered in earlier days from the desire to be perfect parents. We discovered that parents with unrealistic expectations for themselves usually raise kids who feel they never quite measure up either—a crushing burden to place on a child. If we couldn't meet our own high standard, how could our children possibly do it themselves? Perhaps we worried too much about being successful parents, a common mistake.

"We expect certain things from our maturing children," writes Terry Beck, mother of teens. "Unfortunately, we too often measure the quality of our parenting against these expectations. When our expectations are met, we rate our parenting as successful. When our expectations are thwarted, we become angry or frustrated with our children." And who needs another reason to do that? Terry continues, "As our offspring grow in knowledge and independence, we clash over issues that have little importance other than how their behavior in dealing with the issues reflects on us as parents." [5] A huge pothole indeed.

Lynn came downstairs ready for school wearing an old flannel shirt she'd borrowed from a friend. Since she began high school, it seemed every morning she looked messier than the day before. Her hair hung down straight and stringy, the hem of her baggy pants dragging behind worn tennis shoes. It really grated on her well-groomed mother's nerves.

"Why don't you try to look nice any more? Can't you do anything with that hair, and where did you get that awful outfit?" What had happened to the beautiful daughter she had always been so proud of?

Thankfully, Lynn's mom found an approachable moment when her daughter spilled her deep anguish over an increasing weight problem. The messy clothes were merely a cover-up for her own insecurity in a new school environment. Her mother then joined her team as a friend and helper rather than a critic.

Parents who recognize their strong need for perfection can learn to temper it with love and grace before their children are wounded by redirecting their focus from pleasing two imperfect people—themselves—to pleasing one perfect and loving Heavenly Father. The difference is that when Jesus Christ, God the Son, tells us to "be perfect, therefore, as your Heavenly Father is perfect" (Matt. 5:48), He enables us to do that through the indwelling Holy Spirit. God never asks us to do anything without actually walking alongside giving us the power to do it.

When parents demonstrate humility and a real desire to please God, young adults see an example worth modeling. What a relief to realize it is no longer so important that my children reach my imperfect standard, but rather that they learn to please God on their own. The best way to help them do that is to let go of my own private desired outcomes and let God be God.

My dear friend Linda, our pastor's wife, loves to quip, "God loves you and I have wonderful plans for your life." I get nervous whenever she says that because she invariably has big plans in the works. As parents we aren't much different, are we? How about releasing all of our secret dreams for our children to God, and let Him keep the good and blow away the rest like chaff? Then watch and pray and be amazed at the plans He has for them!

Just Thinking

This is a great opportunity for dialogue with your teen. Talk about this list of potholes as a family and find out which ones you may be dangerously near. Perhaps you've already fallen into a deep one. Don't be afraid to call for help. A pastor or family counselor can give you just the lift you need.

è.

CHAPTER EIGHT

Creating strength out of struggles: how to help your kids avoid entanglements

*I*t was already past my bedtime when I quietly opened the front door after a late meeting one cold Tuesday night in January. I knew the children would all be asleep and half expected Steve to be, too. Hearing a crackling fire in the family room, I walked in to find Steve waiting for me.

"Sit down," he said, motioning to the rocker. "Remember when I told you once not to be surprised at anything?" he began. He seemed too calm, too controlled. Having grown up in a family of six children, Steve was almost shock-proof. "Well, this is what I meant. The police were here tonight."

Police, I thought to myself. *That meant there was an accident.* "What happened? Who's been hurt?" I demanded, panic rising quickly inside of me.

"No one's been hurt, at least not physically. It seems our son knowingly bought some stolen merchandise at school and didn't return it. It was that portable CD player we've been questioning him about. Tonight the police found the boy who had stolen it, and the kid told them where everything was. They came to claim it."

A rush of relief and confusion swirled together in my mind. *What does this mean? How serious is this? Why did he do that?* It seemed like a bad dream. Was Steve really telling me this about our son? He was almost a model kid—polite, respectful, honest, and a Christian. How could he do such a stupid thing? Why did he ever get involved?

"How did he react? What did he have to say for himself? What did the police say? What's going to happen to him now?" I blurted out. Suddenly a horrible dark cloud hung over the future. Could this one gross misjudgment leave him with a permanently marred record, not to mention loss of friendships and his good standing at school? He was only fourteen! I could hardly process it all.

"The police officer was really harsh with him," Steve went on. "He hardly spoke to me, but really laid it on the line that purchasing stolen goods was also breaking the law. If he were one year older, he could be in serious trouble."

Later, my son confessed, "Mom, I wanted that CD player so badly. I didn't think it was that wrong to buy it if I hadn't stolen it, but I knew God thought it was wrong. When I saw the police car pull in our driveway, I started sweating and shaking and crying all at once. I thought I'd have a nervous breakdown on the way down the stairs. It was the worst moment of my life."

My son was sorrowful and depressed for months. He didn't lose his friends, but he was deeply humbled before them and before God. It was a long time before he could forgive himself, but was completely cured, I think, of ever breaking the law again. Much like a vaccination, as Howard Hendricks has said, this little bit of the "disease" was enough to prevent him from contracting the real thing.

As parents, we are not always so fortunate to have a problem that can be remedied that easily. Many wonderful loving moms and dads have heard

* "I'm pregnant."
* "If you haven't guessed yet, I'm gay."
* "I've had an abortion."
* "Your daughter has been caught cheating at school and supplying younger students with the answers."
* "Your son has been in a serious accident. Drugs were found in his car."

WHAT'S REALLY GOING ON HERE?

Not only do parents think these nightmares could never happen to *their* child, but most young adults think they are invulnerable, too. In a recent survey of high-achieving high school students conducted by Who's Who Among American High School Students, some alarming statistics emerged:

* Seventy-eight percent admitted they had cheated on a test, quiz, homework, or writing assignment.
* One in five of the females had been a victim of a sexual assault, in most instances by someone she knew.
* One in three knew someone who had brought a weapon to school.
* Forty-two percent of the males had access to one or more firearms.
* More than half reported frequent fights between students. Five percent said there had been a shooting on school grounds and 7.3 percent reported a knife fight.
* One-third considered suicide.[1]

In case these statistics sound like problems facing inner-city students, note that these results were tabulated from the responses of nearly two thousand outstanding students across the board in American high schools in 1993.

It's easy to describe the way things are today. It doesn't take much insight to see the crumbling family unit with its accompanying erosion of faith and values. The media exerts a powerful, relentless pull. Virginity is becoming a novel concept even among young teens. In the local elementary school where I worked last year, a fifth grader admitted being sexually active. What shocked me most was that her teacher wasn't surprised.

So afraid are school districts of lawsuits, that they communicate only a vague system of values at best. Many Christian families have withdrawn their children from the public school environment in order to protect them from the temptations there, only to discover the same problems exist in many Christian schools, also.

Parents are having a tougher time supervising their teens. They're seldom home. It's taking two incomes in most families just to keep from going under financially. The desire for *things* is so powerful that we've become accustomed to a lifestyle and an economy that demand to be fed, like a tapeworm, more and more every day.

In his book *Raising Positive Kids in a Negative World,* Zig Ziglar put it bluntly:

> I can say with reasonable certainty that when your child is between the ages of nine and fifteen, you will have a better chance of losing him to drugs and immorality than at any other stage of his life. During these critical years children are going through many physiological and psychological changes. At the same time they're being bombarded with the moral values of the media, their peer group, family, church, and school. Many of these are often in direct conflict and create considerable confusion within the children's minds as to which values are real and which are artificial.[2]

If the experts like Zig Ziglar and many others are right, and I believe they are, what can parents do to help their children avoid the nasty entanglements with alcohol, drugs, promiscuity, and possessive friendships that derail so many young adult lives? We can do plenty, but it takes commitment. Our strongest line of defense is loving involvement, encouraging healthy activities, and concerted prayer.

THREE WAYS TO HELP YOUR KIDS AVOID ENTANGLEMENTS

1. Get Involved in Their Lives

When our children are small, we are by necessity involved in every area of their lives from breakfast choices to brushing their teeth. Thankfully, they do grow up and need us far less. We transfer responsibility for their personal grooming, daily chores, and such to them. But if we think they really need us less at this point, we are sadly mistaken.

Older children and young adults also need a high degree of parent involvement, but of a different sort. They need to feel loved, appreciated, needed, and prayed for. They need parents who give them real responsibility and show them adult levels of respect as they learn to handle it. Even asking our teenagers' advice and listening attentively makes a tremendous difference in our relationship with them.

Josh McDowell in his book *Right from Wrong* suggests a few questions to help you determine that. "How do you determine the depth and breadth of your relationship with a child or teenager? Try asking:

When's the last time you laughed together?

When's the last time you cried together?

Do you know what his favorite (current) song is?

Do you know who she sits with in the school cafeteria?

When did she last seek your advice?

When did you last forget or cancel a commitment to him?

Do you more often ask questions of or make statements to her?

Have you recently admitted a mistake or fault to him?

What do you know—really know—about her spiritual life?[3]

This provides a good place to begin, but it can be a tough jolt for many of us. When I realized how little I knew about my youngest son's life, it scared me. To enter his world, I learned something about auto mechanics. If I hadn't, I would have continued a bad pattern of little or no involvement at a time when our relationship was hanging by only a thread of love. I may not know much, but now I can sound like a real "motor head" when he and I talk cars.

Using touch to show genuine affection to teens communicates what words often lack. But when your child is leaning in a direction that has you concerned, tensions can make affection difficult to express.

Margie Lewis in her book *The Hurting Parent* emphasizes the need to keep on hugging and expressing love to our children, regardless of how old or prickly they become. She puts it this way:

> One of the most overlooked means of expressing love to young adult children is physical affection. Most of us hand out plenty of this when our kids are young. But as they grow up, we hesitate to express much if any of the intimacy we provided when they were small. And as the differences and hurts separate us, it gets easier and easier to curtail all physical contacts. Yet psychologists tell us every human being craves and needs physical affection. A kiss, a hug, a gentle squeeze, a soft touch on the arm can speak powerfully and eloquently of love.[4]

When you're dealing with a difficult person of any age, even a pat on the shoulder can be a major effort. Why? Simply because our own feelings of hurt, rejection, or anger give us ample reason not to. Margie says showing affection is more than just a feeling, ". . . it's a conscious choice. And sometimes when the feelings sag, it may be mostly resolve. It is as much a matter of mind and will as of the heart."[5]

We need to be creative. Steve used to practice a clever combination of hugs and wrestling holds on our boys when they thought a hug from Dad was "corny."

"How's it going today? How are those big muscles of yours?" he'd say as he grabbed one of them by the arm or shoulders and gave an affectionate squeeze. Invariably this would turn into a playful contest to see if they were stronger than Dad yet.

Having grown up in a quiet family where no one wrestled and we only listened to show tunes or classical music, I never understood the difference between good old-fashioned horse play and fighting.

"Watch out! Watch the coffee table! Someone's going to get hurt!" I'd shriek, leaping around the room, thinking I could prevent certain injury. Finally, I'd just give up and leave the room, or go for a walk to hold onto my sanity.

"You just don't understand, Mom," the guys would chide me later, "It's a 'man thing.'"

How come they look so beet-faced, exhausted, and happy at the same time? I'd wonder. The gleam in Steve's eye said, "Trust me." And I knew the struggler just got hugged.

2. Keep 'Em Busy with Good Stuff

A young adult whom I respect and admire was heavily involved with drugs as a teenager. He's now married and a maturing Christian. I asked him how he would prevent his own children from making the same choices he had made.

"I'd keep them busy with healthy activities, lots of them, especially youth group. I'd encourage their friendships and social life to revolve more around youth group than school, as much as possible."

What do you do if your church doesn't have a good youth group? Find one. If you can't do that, start one. Josh McDowell says youth groups are one of the strongest ways to communicate real truth to our young people: "A healthy and vibrant youth group is an important part of a young person's life—especially for a child from a single-parent home. Meet with your church youth worker and share the progress of your child's spiritual and emotional growth."[6] It is the chief way single moms and dads can bridge the social and relational gaps left by death and divorce. I grew up in a small town in a single-parent family, and our church youth group filled huge holes in my life that my mother couldn't have addressed.

Our own teen's youth group was outrageous fun every Saturday night. Volunteer leaders, Bruce and Cathy Baker, invested every funny brain cell they had in planning creative, well-orchestrated events followed by Bible study, personal sharing, and prayer time. Having attended once, teens seldom missed the next get-together.

Developing sports and music talents, volunteering in community service, baby-sitting, working on a school theater production, riding horses and keeping their stables clean, and doing yard work are healthy ways for young adults to invest hours beyond their studies. Personally, we nixed excessive television and movie viewing, video games, MTV (yuk!), and just "hangin' out" listening to who knows what on the radio. There are better things to do for hours at a time.

The emphasis in this book is on releasing your teenagers into their adult lives. Although it's not my intention to talk about how to make your teens hold the line, it still must be done in the most reasonable, loving but firm way possible. If punishments must be given, they should be explained with respect, mutually agreed upon between husband and wife, and never arbitrary. It's still your house, and as long as your children are under your roof or your financial umbrella, they should live by your rules. Just knowing what parents expect is enough to help many teens avoid entanglements. The strength of our relational love-bond with our teens protects them when other reasoning might waver.

3. Pray Like Mad

Undergirding all our efforts to love and launch our teens is prayer. When one of our teenagers was going through a painful struggle, I went to an older Christian friend for advice. She told me an illustration of prayer I will never forget.

"Do you remember the time Jesus healed the paralytic who was lowered through the roof by four of his friends?" she said. "Well, when we feel too weak to pray for ourselves or our loved ones, we need the help of four trusted friends who will pray like mad for us and not give up until we receive our answer. Now, do you have four friends like that? I will be one of them."

A POWERFUL PRAYER

Jesus knew long ago that a pagan world and its values would try to undo us. He knew the warfare would be intense. Some of the most tender words in the entire Bible are found in Jesus' heartfelt prayer for His disciples just prior to His arrest and crucifixion.

"Holy Father, protect them by the power of your name—the name you gave me—so that they may be one as we are one. While I was with them, I protected them and kept them safe by that name you gave me. None has been lost except the one doomed to destruction so that the Scripture would be fulfilled. . . .My prayer is not that you take them out of the world but that you protect them from the evil one."

— John 17:11–12, 15

We quickly asked three other trusted friends to pray for our struggling teen each day and not give up until we had the answer. They claimed God's promises and interceded in ways we had become too muddled and emotional to do ourselves. Gradually, our spiritual muscles gained strength, and we began to see answers to their prayers until our child was at last standing stronger. It's been a few years now, but I have a feeling our four friends still pray for that child every day. Who can measure the eternal impact of those prayers?

Satan's principal targets are our children, regardless of how hard we may try to protect them, but God has promised to keep them safe through the power of Jesus' name.

In spite of all the emphasis in this chapter on loving involvement, keeping our teens busy with healthy activities and concerted prayer, the reality is there are no quick fixes or easy solutions when your child struggles with entanglements.

The road ahead may be rough and you may move through deeper lessons on releasing than you ever wanted to know. If that's the case, buckle up. And remember, you're never alone.

JUST THINKING

Ask yourself a few hard questions. Taking a look at the ways your teen spends his or her time, are there activities that may lead to future entanglements? Could you be overlooking danger signals now? Is your own willingness to be involved, to make sacrifices of time, money, and convenience holding back healthier involvements like youth group, sports, or mutual hobbies? It's never too late to take apart an old Chevy!

Do you know four trusted prayer partners who will agree to pray daily for your teen? Perhaps you can pray for theirs!

The hidden blessings of failure: making the great discovery that all is not lost

I will change your name,
You shall no longer be called
Wounded, outcast, lonely or afraid.
I will change your name.
Your new name shall be
Confidence, joyfulness,
Overcoming one, faithfulness,
Friend of God,
One who seeks my face.
– Song by D. J. Butler[1]

Life can hurt so badly at times. Last night I received a phone call from a distraught mother whose son had just been arrested for possession of drugs. I listened as she described the heartbreak and disillusionment she and her husband felt at the shocking news.

———

"My husband and I both cried," she said. "I've never seen him sob like that. What do we do now? After all we've done to try and be good Christian parents, it feels like my son's life is going down the tubes!"

There was a time when Steve and I thought our son's life was going down the tubes, too. I felt her pain like it was my own and promised her we'd be in prayer that God would show His mighty power in their family situation. This chapter is dedicated to the encouragement of these hurting parents and others like them.

THE REAL VALUE OF FAILURE

Failure. Even the word spells judgment, usually self-imposed. Personal failure brings even the toughest of us to our knees. How easily parents point the finger at their own failed parenting when their children falter and turn aside from the better path. Yet failure can be one of God's most powerful tools for remaking the inner person and birthing a ministry that would otherwise have been impossible. Failure makes us humble, real, and relatable to others—something success cannot do.

Jeffery Jernigan, employee relations manager with Focus on the Family, often shares his own trek through the muck of failure with fellow employees:

I think we view maturity and success as the lack of struggle in life rather than as the process of struggling well. Such thinking leaves us ill-equipped to cope with the reality of failure. Failure, however, can be one of life's best teachers. Often our best lessons come from the "school of hard knocks." I've often wondered why Jesus, the perfect Teacher, the Master who knew everything, didn't give his disciples all the answers. Perhaps it was because, like us, the disciples needed to spend a lifetime in the "school of hard knocks."[2]

I've often wondered why Jesus doesn't give us all the answers, too. Could it be that our "struggling well" is where real permanent change occurs? When our children pass through a season of personal agony, or put us through one, it seems a terrible mistake. A. B. Davidson, respected Scottish Bible scholar of a century ago, suggests our view may be too small: "Those who have exercised the greatest influence on the world have worked long in the dark, struggling with themselves. Disappointments, defeats, repulses, are the education of strong natures."[3]

FAMILIES WHO OVERCAME FAILURE

Overcoming failure can be the doorway to a fulfilling life and a powerful ministry. Hearing stories of young people who have done more than survive, rather have received a wonderful new life by faith, is a great encouragement to parents who wonder if it will ever happen to their wandering child.

Matt and Christa's Story

Within the past year and a half, two weddings created a lot of hoopla for our family and friends. They were victory celebrations for several sets of praying parents, a team of faithful friends, and a host of worn-out angels. The stories that preceded these weddings have proved to many that there is no challenge too big for God, no failure that cannot be redeemed, no life that He won't move mountains to restore. I've come to believe that the bigger the problem, the more God delights in solving it. Our part is learning to pray "big enough." Let me tell you the stories behind the wedding bells.

Matt was a star athlete in high school, well-known throughout the area as a champion wrestler and football player. His prospects for his dream, a football scholarship at Penn State, looked promising.

Matt's parents had provided a stable, loving Christian home and were leaders of the church youth group. On his high school campus, Matt led a teen Bible study and was a strong witness for Christ. Handsome, popular, and personable, Matt had everything any guy could want, including a beautiful girlfriend, Christa, whom he had led to Christ. They were the last two people anyone expected to become parents at sixteen. I asked them what their reaction was to the news.

"I think I was in denial," Christa said. "I kept missing my period and thinking, 'It must be something else. I couldn't be pregnant.' We had only 'done it' once, but after missing it three times, I finally told Matt. He went absolutely white."

Christa wondered if she should have an abortion. She was so young to have a baby. The night she decided to go ahead with it, she felt life for the first time. Christa knew she had to give the baby a chance.

Matt's parents were loving, helpful, and supportive, even offering to let Christa stay with them, but still they worried about future plans. Matt's dad asked him one day, "If Christa weren't pregnant right now, would you still be dating her?"

"Yes," Matt responded thoughtfully, voicing an admission that gave him peace about their future together. They decided to wait to get married until after high school graduation, but the biggest conflicts were still a few months away when their daughter, Brianna, was born.

"It was the worst time for me," Christa shared honestly. "I never slept more than three or four hours a night. Matt's mom watched the baby for me while I was at school, but then I'd come home, take care of her, do my studies, and then be up at night, too. I was exhausted and depressed for months. My biggest mistake was not letting anyone help me. I kept insisting I had to do it all myself." Worse yet, she and Matt weren't getting along at all.

"We hardly spoke to each other for months," Matt confessed. "I should have taken more of the responsibility rather than making her do it all herself. I went out with my friends all the time. I only invited her once, and if she said 'No,' I went out anyway. My friends were as important as Christa was. That part of the whole period was about the worst."

It felt like an eternity to Matt and Christa and their families, but after several months, things finally began to change. Matt's parents learned to give them the space they needed to talk, even argue, and tensions began to melt.

"Once I started getting some sleep, my depression lifted," Christa said. "I knew that I loved Matt more than anyone, except God. By the time our senior year came, we were engaged and I just wanted to get married."

Matt's life began to turn around when an older friend asked him how Christa and the baby were. He realized how long it had been since he'd spent any time with them at all. "I knew it was time to begin to work on my relationships. I had to learn to think of my family now."

When asked how God has changed them through this experience, Christa answered, "I don't know what I'd be doing now if this hadn't happened. I guess I'd be off in college somewhere. In my eyes, things are as good now as they could have been if we'd gotten married the right way, which would have been better in the Lord's eyes. Our sin is forgiven. I know it was wrong and I can help people that way. Telling them what I went through, they can see what God can do for anybody."

Matt and Christa now live in married student housing while Matt is a student at college training to be a teacher and, no doubt, a coach. Beautiful, blue-eyed, curly-haired Brianna will certainly charm the whole campus. Looking down at her, Christa can hardly believe she once considered abortion. She envisions working with teenagers one day in a crisis pregnancy center, in addition to speaking with Matt to youth groups about the dangers of premarital sex.

"We always bring pictures of Brianna when we speak to kids," Matt adds. "One of the biggest things I'm looking forward to is public speaking. At a camp I went to as a teenager, I stood up and said that I was willing to be a speaker for Christ. That kind of took a back seat in my life for awhile. Now that all this has happened to me . . . I have something to speak about, so I think the Lord has brought me full circle."

Listening to Matt and Christa, watching their love enfold one another and little Brianna, I feel enriched. I know I won't be the only one.

Bob and Theresa's Story

The next story is different but points to the relentless love and faithfulness of God. I am indebted to our son Bob and his wife, Theresa, for allowing me to share it with you.

Our home was one that spawned a rebel, an increasingly common theme. Bob is the youngest of our four, adopted at nineteen months after his parents' untimely death. We had prayed for a little brother for Dave, and knew God brought Bob to us. He was smart, cute, and tough, with enough energy for several toddlers all rolled into one. Strong-willed by nature, soon it became clear that Bob felt confined by even the smallest rules and put his toe across every line we drew. Many days he completely wore us out.

By the time Bob reached fourteen or fifteen, problems at home and at school were accelerating. Steve and I were the recipients of his increasing anger whenever limits were placed on the total freedom he felt he deserved. We approached his problem with anger from every angle we could think of— including counseling, overlooking as much negative behavior as we could, reinforcing all the good we could find at the time, direct confrontation and consequences related to outright defiance. We even tried lowering our standards, wondering if we just expected too much. But after a few years of this, it wasn't hard to see the family begin to go under.

I worried daily that Steve might have a heart attack from the stress of dealing with a rebel, coupled with an enormously demanding job. Teachers at school began calling home about signs of undue stress in our other children. My blood pressure rose and I needed medication. It was a long and difficult time for all of us, including our rebellious son.

Rebels usually feel that they are the only ones hurting. Their own pain and confusion boxes in their world smaller and smaller until they are the only ones who can fit inside. It's an intensely self-centered time—one that many look back on later as adults with deep regret.

My friend Ginnie Olsen had a godly mother who has since packed up her earthly life and moved to heaven. Ginnie's mom said so many wise and wonderful things, I wish I had a book of them. One that I often repeated to my kids was, "Anyone all wrapped up in himself makes a pretty small package!" That's certainly true of all of us at different times in our lives, but seldom as true as it is for the rebel. It's a hurtful time in a home, but one of the toughest side effects is that very often it is also misunderstood by everyone outside the home, as well. Ruth Bell Graham knows the feeling well:

> *They felt good eyes upon them*
> *and shrank within—undone;*
> *good parents had good children*
> *and they—a wandering one.*
> *The good folk never meant*
> *to act smug or condemn,*
> *but having prodigals*
> *just "wasn't done" with them.*
> *Remind them gently, Lord,*
> *how You*
> *have trouble with Your children,*
> *too.*[4]

One night, after a major confrontation, Steve held Bob firmly by the shoulders and said, "Bob, I love you, but I can't let you tear the family apart. You have to treat others decently and respect the rules. You've got to choose how you are going to live if you are going to live here." And choose he did, but not the choices we wanted him to make. One week before his seventeenth birthday, Bob chose to leave home and live with relatives in another city.

Steve said recently, "One of the worst nights of my life was driving Bob there. The road home was so lonely I could hardly bear it. After all the effort I had put into being a good dad, I felt I had failed completely."

DEALING WITH PARENTAL GUILT

When your child's life caves in, it's natural to point the finger at yourself and say, "I must have been a terrible parent or this wouldn't have happened! What did I do that was so wrong, so detrimental to bring about this response?"

Steve and I asked ourselves these haunting questions day and night, pleading with God to make clear our failures so we could confess them, ask our son's forgiveness, and then everything could get better. No clear answer came.

Barbara Johnson is a mother well acquainted with feelings of failure and grief. Two of her sons died young, one in Vietnam and the other killed by a drunk driver. When her third son announced he was gay and disappeared into a lifestyle that was personally repugnant to her, she fell apart completely. Barbara has experienced much emotional healing and has seen her third son restored to a healthy lifestyle and walk with the Lord. She has this to say about undue guilt: "Parents are always asking, 'Where did I go wrong?' I tell them that God was a perfect parent, and look at the big mess He had with Adam! Who are we to think that we can be parents and not have big problems with our kids, too?"[5]

No one can grieve with you like another parent who's "been there." What a comfort it was to know God had "been there," too. He understood our feelings of failure and didn't hold them against us. We wondered, "If God isn't making us feel guilty, who is?"

Deciding What Matters

When moving through a crisis with a young person, parents need to decide what matters and what does not. Steve and I came to the conclusion that only three things really mattered: preserving the home, restoring the child, and pleasing God. It did not matter what other people thought. It would be impossible for them to understand unless they had been through something very similar anyway.

Preserving the Home

When home becomes a place where family members can no longer live normally and safely, it's time to make some adjustments. Bill Hybels lays it right on the line:

> Peace at any price is a form of deception from the pit of hell. When you know you need to tell the truth, the evil one whispers in your ear, 'Don't do it. He won't listen. She won't take it. It will blow up in your face. It will cause too much hurt. It will only make things worse. It's not worth it.' If you believe those lies, there is a high probability that you will kill your relationship sooner or later. . . . Tough love chooses truth telling over peace keeping and trusts God for the outcome.[6]

Truth telling means facing reality head on. Simply stated, there are consequences for sin which may mean radical adjustments to life as we have always known it. For Matt and Christa, it meant shouldering the responsibilities of marriage and parenthood years earlier than they had planned. For Bob, it meant moving out of the house. For parents, it means the most costly form of loving they've ever experienced.

Restoring the Child

It's important for the hurting teenager to feel understood, to be listened to if he or she is willing to talk. We need to communicate to our son or daughter that, no matter what he has done, our love hasn't changed. God specializes in putting His children back together with forgiveness and grace when they fall. He has surprising ways of keeping His promise in 1 Peter 5:10: "And the God of all grace, who called you to his eternal glory in Christ, after you have suffered a little while, will himself restore you and make you strong, firm and steadfast." Picture the God of the universe restoring your child, making him "strong, firm and steadfast." God's purpose is infinitely more loving and far-reaching than our own desires to just "get through this." He is building a difference-maker.

Bob's restoration began on a night when he had hit bottom. One evening, he borrowed a friend's motorcycle and drove it a hundred miles an hour hoping to crash and end all his problems. When he couldn't crash it, he stopped at a local market to get something to eat. Theresa was just coming out of the market with friends who stopped to talk with Bob. One look at her gave Bob a reason for living again.

God used Theresa like an angel in Bob's life, listening to him, offering another perspective, helping him face his anger over the events God had allowed in his life. Little by little, the anger and rebellion dissolved.

Pleasing the Lord

Is it possible to please the Lord while dealing with problems like teenage pregnancy, or taking such drastic action as to ask a child to shape up or ship out? That's a tough question for any parent. We found these steps critical:

Examine your own heart and actions honestly before the Lord. It's easy to push our children over the edge of reasonable behavior when we neglect them emotionally by not spending enough time listening to them, by setting boundaries that are either too lax or too stringent and not releasing them gradually into adult life, or by criticizing and ridiculing them rather than accepting the natural personality and abilities God has given him or her.

If any of these are the case, before you do anything else, ask God's forgiveness for your own failings. We have only our pride to lose, which is a very good thing to be rid of, and worlds of good to gain. Next, you need to ask your child's forgiveness regardless of his or her response. The world is full of wounded adults whose parents could never bring themselves to say "I'm sorry" and mean it. Get the record clean so that you can be ready to receive God's guidance with the problem at home.

Commit yourself to Christian counseling, if it is available. If the problem is of a more clinical, serious nature, seek a well-recommended professional whose values are in agreement with yours. We've seen God use secular counselors in very helpful ways. Try to go as a family, remembering that this is a problem involving all the family, not just one member. If your child won't go, go alone. Just go!

Ask several trusted friends to pray. Daily prayer for your family, for your hurting and miserable child, and for wisdom for you is essential, but don't use those relationships in any way that will compromise your child's trust. People who love you don't need to know every confidence or private family matter. They can pray effectively anyway.

"How's it going?" my friend Judie often asked, squeezing my hand as we met at church.

"Oh, not too good. On a scale of 1 to 10, our son's a 2 today and we're a minus 2. Just pray for us!"

I remember one afternoon with my friends Judie and Lorraine lingering over coffee in the waning sunlight of Lorraine's dining room. I began to share my deep concerns for Bob when a wave of tears made it impossible to continue. In the quiet that followed, both women bowed their heads and wept with me, lovingly lifting our family's needs to our Heavenly Father in prayer. Friends whom we allow to share our grief will also share in our super-joy when God answers.

Learn to change your focus from centering on "the problem child" to centering on pleasing God. Recognize that God is with you all the time. He is reading your heart and thoughts as well as your child's, and His goal is for everyone to learn to think, love, and act as He does. Make it your goal to turn from every word or action that will leave you ashamed later. This is very tough in the heat of difficulty, but with grace and Christ in your heart, you can do it.

Give the outcome to God. Thank Him for all the wonderful purposes He has that you can't see now, and then trust Him if the roof falls in, no matter what happens. God is never unkind to us, even though it may seem so at the time.

Matt's parents' decision to trust God with their son's future gave him the responsibility to work out his priorities regarding Christa and their daughter. The hardest thing parents ever do is learn, as Jan Silvious reminds us, to "back up, pray up, and shut up."

Last, give God elbow room to act, even in the middle of your mess. Take time to pray, seek godly counsel from others and from the Scriptures, and always act in agreement with your spouse. If the situation is totally out of your hands, place it in God's hands. Release all the authority and power to Him and then trust Him to make good on all the promises you claim, like this wonderful one in Psalm 126:5–6:

> Those who sow in tears
>   will reap with songs of joy.
> He who goes out weeping,
>   carrying seed to sow,
> will return with songs of joy,
> carrying sheaves with him.

Our song of joy came at the rehearsal dinner for Bob and Theresa's wedding. Steve placed his arms around them both and prayed for them with all the families present. It was a moment to cherish. Steve thanked God for the wonderful work He had done in Bob's life, for making him a man of strength who keeps his word, who works faithfully and honorably, and one who seeks a godly heritage. He thanked Him especially for Theresa, for the depth of her love for Bob and for the joy she has brought to his life and ours, and he asked God to bless them both with a life of love and service to Him.

Only one year before, we had shared the same joy at Matt and Christa's wedding reception, watching them dance with Brianna in their arms.

When God restores, He restores beyond our dreams. I'm learning not to be surprised at all the wonderful things He is doing—just very thankful. I now look toward the future with trust and enthusiasm. By faith, you can, too.

JUST THINKING

If you are moving through a season of difficulty with your son or daughter, sit down with your spouse, or with a pastor or close friend if you are single, and decide what really matters. What does your young adult need most from God and from you as a parent? Write it down, put a date on it, and refer to it every day as you pray for him. Ask God for a promise from His Word that will carry you through and bring hope and encouragement where it is needed.

Next, work through each of the six steps mentioned above under "Pleasing the Lord." Make it your whole aim to please God in the little things and trust Him with the big ones. Thank Him that He holds both you and your much-loved child in the palm of His hand.

ॐ

Letting Go

CHAPTER TEN

Parents who warm God's heart: five ways to reflect His love

Many years ago there was a family with six children who lived in a small town in very humble circumstances. The father was known throughout the town as a man of integrity, often working two or three jobs to provide for his family. The mother sewed, ironed, baked, and cooked from sunup until sundown with such an uncomplaining attitude that the children seldom realized what a hardship this was for her. The three older boys often came home with a friend or two from high school and devoured a whole loaf of homemade bread and jam at one sitting, never realizing the lack it might create.

Yet they were richer than most. The children often heard their parents giggle and talk downstairs at night, peeked through heavy draperies at weddings in the parlor conducted by their dad—the local justice of the peace—ate homemade cinnamon rolls for breakfast and picnicked on Sundays after church with a herd of cousins at the extended family's farm. They were loved and God was good. It was enough.

Still, it would seem an unlikely place to turn for extra space needed by a much poorer boy whose home had burned. Things were already far too tight.

"He can have my bed," said the eldest, himself a polio victim. "I'll use the couch. We'll take turns." The parents must have wondered how seven children and two adults would fit into a small house with only one bathroom. The three little girls already shared one big bed. There was no room! What about meals, laundry, the endless ironing?

"OK. He can stay," was the response without hesitation, met with cheers from the others. Did any of these young givers count the cost? Did those parents ever imagine the power of their example, the hope poured back into one hopeless young man? Could they have known then how his love for them would become a heart of gratefulness to God, how he would learn to believe in himself and achieve greatness and honor in his profession, how he would be marked by their love? Could they have known that those who watched and learned and sacrificed space and place would also be enriched by those years to become givers themselves?

I know. I married one of them and his quiet generosity has amazed me over our nearly thirty years of marriage. How do children learn to be givers? They learn it at home.

In the writing of this book I have had a keener sense of all the ways I wished I'd loved more, listened more, played more, helped more during the years we were raising our children. But one thing Steve and I both did was to pray for guidance, for love, mercy, and forgiveness, but most of all, for wisdom. And we watched for His answers.

Many of them came through other parents who were carefully observed through the windows of our world. I cherished their example and was touched by the ways they resonated a Father's kind of love.

PARENTS WHO GIVE

You'd think once your five children were raised, you'd want nothing more to do with the stresses of parenting. Why would you volunteer to help with huge groups of rowdy teenagers at youth group, then yearly act as chaperones, referees, and stand-in grandparents on retreats, being coerced into playing broom ball in the freezing cold, counseling a rebel late into the night, and then inviting them all for a home-cooked meal and a daylong mini-retreat at your house one month later? Hard for this new empty-nester to fathom, but that's what Gary and Lorraine Slighter have been doing for almost twenty years. An entire generation of young adults has been touched by their example. I am so thankful our four were among them.

Recently Amy reminisced on the phone, "I used to go into Mrs. Slighter's kitchen and listen to her tell me all about the things she had made for us: big pans of lasagna, sometimes even turkey or roast beef. She would let us fix a drink whenever we wanted one. It was so free. Every room of their house was open to us, nothing was held back, especially when we played team games in groups. We spread out all over their upstairs."

The Slighter's ministry to young people included a form of mentoring. They propagated other couples who made giving look effortless, opening their homes to teens for outrageous fun and great food, at the same time providing an atmosphere for discussion and personal growth. Young adults saw firsthand that the biblical model for loving relationships truly works.

Gary and Lorraine taught a standard for confidentiality that many church leaders would do well to imitate: If kids told them something, it never went any further, ever! Not even to parents or pastors. They were absolutely safe to talk to, but the burdens they carried in prayer were often crushing.

Bill Hybels, pastor of the burgeoning Willow Creek Church, talks about this kind of giver in his book *Who You*

Are (When No One's Looking): "I have found that love is a lot more closely related to work than to play. It has a lot more to do with being a servant than with being a hero . . . .When I set about the task of loving, I usually end up giving instead of receiving. Love inevitably costs me something, usually the three commodities most precious to me—my time, my energy and my money."[1]

One thing Steve and I learned from Gary and Lorraine and those like them is that real giving is very costly, but it's an investment in God's family that brings Him great joy. He uses our arms to reach out and rescue young people who are dangerously close to losing hope. We are the ones to lead and welcome home those He has been drawing.

PARENTS WHO PRAY

"Hi! Come on in!" Gordon threw open the door and helped us off with our coats. It was "pizza and prayer night" but it felt like a party. The Tucker's kitchen and family room were full of parents in comfortable old clothes, some sitting on the floor by the woodstove, others engaged in conversation in the kitchen. At the table Gordon's wife, Lorraine, was putting together a large salad and lining up box after box of steaming pizza! What a feast!

In a little while everyone had gathered in the family room to share the special needs of more than thirty college students. Splitting up into groups of four or five around the house, parents prayed nearly an hour for every college student we knew, and even some we didn't know whose names were referred to us. Upon leaving, each person carried a list of several students' names whom they promised to pray for daily until we met again. It was a powerful ministry begun by two moms with a burden for kids away from home.

Can you imagine the far-reaching effect of these prayers? What an important place other parents have in launching our children into their adult lives. Their prayers fuel the launch and provide the power needed for our children's decision making, their protection, courage, spiritual growth, and physical well-being. I can't think of a greater boost to young adults nor their parents than knowing a team of Christian friends is praying for them every day. It's a true reflection of our Heavenly Father's love.

PARENTS WHO TRUST

"Mom and Dad, I'd like to go to a party after the big homecoming game, OK? Everybody's going, all the other cheerleaders and their friends, not to mention all the guys on the football team."

"Where is it being held, Carrie?" her dad asked.

"Well, that's what you may not like. It's going to be over at the sand pits. Now I know what you're thinking. It's going to be a beer party and, yes, I'm sure there will be beer there, but I'm not going to have any. You can trust me to have soda."

"It's not that I don't trust you, but I'm not sure that's the kind of party you should be attending. Why not have some friends over to the house instead?"

"Dad, you always say that! When am I going to be allowed to make my own decisions? I'll be gone next year at college! Why can't you let go of me now?"

"Well," added her mom in a soothing voice, "let's just pray about it a day and then decide, honey."

"I've already prayed about it! I want to go! I wish you'd just trust me!" Carrie turned away from her parents and went red-nosed up to her room. It was becoming a regular theme. Bill and Jen had a hard time letting her go. She was their first, so precious, so vulnerable, and yet so strong at the same time. They felt proud of the woman she was becoming, but the risks seemed too great at times.

Years earlier they had carefully begun training her to make her own decisions. Hadn't she managed things beautifully when her mother had been ill? And think of all the baby-sitting she had done! Several couples already trusted her to take care of their house and children for nearly a week at a time. Why were her own parents having trouble?

There's no greater compliment for a young adult than his parents' trust. By allowing him to make decisions on his own, relinquishing our grip on the outcome, we communicate a form of trust that nothing else can imitate. This kind of releasing begins, of course, years earlier with much smaller issues and builds as responsible behavior grows. Huge issues involving a young person's personal safety or even his repu-tation can hinge on a moment's quick judgment. Training for those moments begins long before.

Bill and Jen decided to take the leap and give her permis-sion to go. After all, Carrie had already proven herself. She deserved their trust and support, but still, it was a difficult decision.

Homecoming weekend came in a flurry of autumn bril-liance. Her parents attended the parade and the big game, trying not to appear worried or anxious as Carrie waved good-bye across the school parking lot and climbed into the backseat of a car full of noisy, laughing seniors. Horns blared a victory celebration, but Bill and Jen rode home in silence.

About eight o'clock that night, headlights flashed in the driveway. A car door slammed and in the back door came Carrie!

"What are you doing home now? Did something go wrong at the party?" her mother asked, surprised at her sudden arrival.

"No. I never went. I had the kids drop me off here after pizza."

"But, why? I thought it was so important for you to go?"

"It was, until you let me decide. But when you let me make my own decision, then I had to be honest with myself. I knew I didn't belong there either."

"Honey, come here," Bill said ruffling his daughter's hair. "You're quite a gal! Quite a gal!"

Have you graduated to that point in parenting where you are learning this kind of trust? Everyone's experience may not turn out as well as this one did, and no doubt Carrie's parents earned a few gray hairs after she left for college, too. But it's a wise parent who learns to exercise trust in his son or daughter while he is still home. It requires allowing room for failure without saying, "I told you so," offering sincere compliments when they've made good judgments, and the kind of guidance in decision making that you'd like to receive in similar circumstances. Being treated with real respect goes miles toward building the kind of character that is *worthy* of respect.

Today Carrie has completed college and works with delinquent boys in the inner city. Suddenly, that party at the sand pits looks pretty tame. Her parents have learned to trust God for their daughter in many difficult circumstances. They have demonstrated that in every circumstance God's promises will hold our full weight and our children's weight at the same time, every time.

One of the most difficult issues Christian parents face is allowing their young person to make the final decision on the choice of a college. It's a common feeling among Christian families that the Christian college environment, at least a year of it, will build lifetime spiritual strength and commitment into their son or daughter. When their children don't want the same thing, the parents are devastated.

What will happen to them at that secular campus? It's so pagan. There's no way my child is living in a coed dorm! They'll come home numb and accepting of the worldly lifestyles and never find a nice Christian to marry! I absolutely won't allow it!

Perhaps it would help these parents to hear from others who have waded through the same secular or Christian college dilemma and lived to tell the story.

One mother of four put it this way: "I expected my oldest daughter to emerge from her Christian college a strong Christian. Frankly, she's a little disillusioned, having met so many uncommitted kids at this college. We expected more. On the other hand, our son went to a local state school for lack of money, and became quickly involved in a campus ministry. He's thinking of going to seminary when he graduates!"

Friends of ours sent their son, with serious misgivings, to a large private university known to be a powerhouse of pagan thinking. He was pretty much "on the fence" with his faith in his first year but was impressed with how closely knit the Christians were on this campus. They had to be tough to survive! Quite honestly, they were the most fun to be with and even had a volunteer band on Friday nights. Their fellowship group was huge and highly organized. Soon he was being discipled regularly by a "big brother" in the Christian group, and, by his junior year, became a Bible study leader himself. For those of us who prayed for him, this young man brought us a lot of joy and no doubt caused a lot of rejoicing in heaven, too.

A former pastor of ours, whose children all attended secular colleges, was truly impressed at the strength of the Christians on these campuses. Having attended college literally on a mission field, they are less disillusioned and more ministry-oriented when they graduate.

In the last analysis, don't be too afraid if God leads your son or daughter to a secular college rather than the Christian college you might choose for them. God is more than able to care for them and provide others to disciple them in surprising ways.

It's much easier to trust the choices your young adult makes when you are regularly in prayer for him and can trust the big God you're talking to. It will help when you receive a call like one mother I know at 7:30 in the morning from her son at college.

"Mom, I'm in love! I've just met the girl I think I'm going to marry!"

"Well, tell me about her. How long have you been dating?"

"About a week, Mom. But remember when you told me you knew Dad was the one you were going to marry after your first date? Well, the same thing happened to me!" And she smiled, mentally kicking herself for telling him that. I have the feeling God was smiling, too.

PARENTS WHO STAND IN THE GAP

"Say, John, if it's all right with you, we'd like to invite your son Danny to stay with us a couple of weeks. We don't want to intrude, but he's been over here with us a lot lately, and well, I know he's been making things pretty miserable for all of you. He seems to be better when he's here. Maybe it would give you all a breather. How about it?"

Under normal circumstances, no parent would volunteer to do this, but behind this father's offer was a bedrock love for both Danny and his worn-out parents. He could see them cracking under the strain and was willing to stand in the gap with a brief respite for everyone to regroup. These are rare folks, ones who listen carefully for God's directives and aren't afraid to take bold steps to obey them. They sometimes don't get to see the results of their obedience, but it doesn't matter. They get the joy inside just from doing it. May God multiply their example.

Kim Pederson was a parent like this. She saw the need for young people to "connect" with an older person other than their parents and began opening her home weekly to a group of local high school girls for a friendly chat and Bible study. One by one over a period of at least two years, these girls made deep personal commitments to Christ. One chose full-time Christian service, and another eventually became Kim's daughter-in-law! What would have been the result had Kim felt she just didn't have time? I recently learned that some ten years later, Kim continues this ministry by discipling a group of girls in New Hampshire. I think when she gets to heaven there will be a whole wing of God's house populated with her "spiritual children"!

Parents who will stand in the gap as friends, surrogate parents, and disciplers are parents who are carefully tuned to God's own heartbeat. Will you and I be ready when He taps us for similar service?

PARENTS WHO COOPERATE WITH GOD

I read an article by Cliff Barrows, music and program director for the Billy Graham Evangelistic Association. His musical talents have blessed millions. In his article, Cliff relates a conversation he had with his dad shortly before he died:

"Dad couldn't see, and he could hardly hear; nor did he recognize my voice. I was the only one in the room that day, and I decided: 'I'm going to ask Dad some questions about 'Cliff.'"

Without his dad recognizing his voice, Cliff asked him about how he felt when Cliff abandoned his father's dream for him to become a surgeon. "What did you and Mrs. Barrows want Cliff to become? What were your ambitions for him?"

Without hesitation he raised both hands and, with a smile, he reminisced, "We wanted him to become a surgeon. We thought that he had good hands and that he would make a good doctor."

"I knew that this was true," writes Cliff, " because . . . the notion was ingrained into me. I wrote term papers about doctors and medicine. . . . I really wanted to become a doctor.

"My aunt had told me, 'I'll send you to the University of California at Berkeley, and I'll pay your way through, if you will study medicine.' I was set for that direction, I thought—until God spoke to my heart."

Turning to his dad again, Cliff asked: "Did Cliff become a surgeon?"

He shook his head, "No . . . he became a song leader for Billy Graham, and he preaches once in a while."

Cliff continues, "Then I asked Dad a leading question: 'Mr. Barrows, were you disappointed? Your aspiration was for Cliff to become a surgeon, and he became a song leader and a minister.'

"Dad waited quite a few seconds and then turned in my direction. With a little smile on his face, he said, 'No. He had to do the will of God.'

"I put my arms around him. 'Dad,' I said, 'this is Cliff speaking to you.'

"He laughed. 'You rascal! You tricked me!'

"As I hugged him, I said, 'Dad, thank you for putting God's will and plan for your children above your own personal desires; you wanted God's will most of all. I will always be proud to tell people about my father. You've set an example for me that I am passing on.'"[2]

Suppose Cliff Barrows's dad had not released his son and given his blessing on his call from God? Or suppose Cliff, out of a sense of love and indebtedness to his parents, had felt obliged to continue his studies to become a doctor? He probably would have made a fine doctor, but I can guarantee he would never have been a happy one. Remembering the advice of an elderly Bible teacher in Baltimore years ago, the only safe path for any of us to follow is the one close behind the Savior's steps.

Incidentally, Cliff Barrows doesn't know my name, but I think he will always remember me as the woman and her daughter on Friday night of the big Capital District Crusade in Albany, New York, who stepped into last-minute seating wearing bright red and green blouses and were accidentally placed in the crisp white rows of the choir. Following the urging of the nice lady to our right who held the music and said, "It's easy. Just stand and sing along with us!" we stood with the choir when Cliff raised his baton. A look of horror and disbelief crossed his face only briefly the moment he looked up. What wonderful composure Cliff Barrows has! Yes, I believe he would have made an excellent surgeon, too.

A RUSTLE OF WINGS

It's almost time for your son or daughter to leave home and try her wings. Or perhaps she's already left and you're struggling with the direction she has chosen. I would encourage you to give her back to God, asking His fullness of blessing and power in her life. Make a monument to your prayer by writing it down in your Bible or prayer journal: "On this day I release my son or daughter to God's care as I have done many times in the past; I now do it one more time for good. Thank you, Lord, for all you are doing to guide, care for, and protect my child."

Barbara Johnson, whose warmth and wisdom have helped me through this process, puts it like this: "We have to give them to God, and then take our hands off. It is like wrapping a package up and putting on a label, and then being able to send it, without our special directions of where to go, but letting God put the address on the label, or on that life. Can you love your child and pray for him and let God do with his life what He wants to do? Minus your instructions?"[3]

That's the rub. As parents who have released their children into adult life, fully committing them to God for His care, direction, protection, and love, we are no longer their personal gurus. We need to cooperate with God by praying for our children earnestly every day, if necessary carrying them hour by hour to the Lord in prayer, but allowing God to speak to them and lead them in His own way, in His own time. Remember it's been said, "Trees that brave storms are not propagated in hot houses!"

JUST THINKING

Think about other parents who exemplified the qualities that most reflect God's heart. As a family, talk about the ways their example has challenged you and your children. Ask your son or daughter, "How has this couple influenced you? In what ways would you like to carry their example into your own home one day?" Why not write them a letter thanking them for their faithfulness? Other young people besides your children may imitate you one day, too.

之

The serendipity of letting go: celebrating the freedom to become

*L*etting go is a bittersweet affair. On one hand, it brings feelings of accomplishment for reaching the goal we've been working toward all these years; our children are finally grown and ready to try their wings in adult life. On the other hand, it's a wrenching from our grasp of the daily feeling of being needed, consulted, laughed with, vitally linked with our son or daughter. The cord must be cut, but it seems painful. Ruth Graham describes her feeling of loss:

> *We live a time*
> *secure;*
> *beloved and loving,*
> *sure*
> *it cannot last*
> *for long*
> *then—*
> *the good-byes come*

again—again—
like a small death,
the closing of a door.
One learns to live with pain.
One looks ahead,
not back—
never back,
only before.
And joy will come again—
warm and secure,
if only for the now,
laughing,
we endure.[1]

A door in life is swinging shut. Unquestionably, there is a period of grief and loss for every parent who finds himself on the quiet side of the door. No matter how well prepared you are for the process of letting go, an unguarded moment will remind you that a piece of your heart is missing.

Dealing with Loss

As Your Kids Leave for College

Dr. Marie Chapian—author, speaker, and counselor—couldn't have prepared herself better for the day she would deposit her daughter in college. She did everything right, only to discover her feelings wouldn't listen to reason. I love her honesty:

> One of the most traumatic days of my life was the day in September when I drove my daughter to college for her first long-term experience away from home. She was accepted at a good Christian college in southern California an hour and a half away. We celebrated—I especially. I was so thrilled for her to be going to college, living in a dorm, the works. . . . And then came the day we drove up to the school.

A sunshiny day, the car packed to the sun roof, singing up the highway as we went. I was beaming with delight at having come to one of life's milestones, a veritable "passage," naive as to what lay in wait for me. We hauled her stuff up to her room, we prayed, I helped her unpack, make her bunk bed—oh, the fun of it all. I was sort of like a bouncing clown, pleased with every little detail of the place: the mom who never got to live in a dorm or go away to private college. It was a dream come true. So we kissed and hugged and I bounced back into the empty car—and then it hit me.

My baby had left me. I felt myself decompose. I cried so hard I had to pull off the interstate. I sat on the beach crying and howling and hyperventilating, because it hit me that this could be it. The big *it*. In only a matter of minutes she was a resident of a new place where she'd be for four years, after which time she may never come home to live permanently again. I suddenly missed her so intensely, so completely that I was consumed with a sort of grief I'd never known. It spread over me in cold, gray dread that her sounds, her face, her voice, the exhilarating conversations, her laughter, her music . . . were gone. [2]

You may think only mothers miss their children that intensely, right? Not so! Listen to James Dobson open his heart after depositing his only son, Ryan, on a plane bound for college: "There I was, driving down the freeway when an unexpected wave of grief swept over me. I thought I couldn't stand to see him go. It was not that I dreaded or didn't look forward to what the future held. No, I mourned the end of an era—a precious time of my life when our children were young and their voices rang in the halls of our house."

Later, piecing his thoughts together, he reflects,

When Ryan boarded that plane in Los Angeles, I comprehended anew the brevity of life and the temporary nature of all things. As I sat on the floor of his room, I heard not only Ryan's voice but the voices of my mother and father who laughed and loved in that place. Now they are gone. One day Shirley and I will join them. First one and then the other. We are just "passing through" as the gospel song-writers used to say. All of life boils down to a series of happy "hellos" and sad "good-byes." Nothing is really permanent, not even the relationships that blossom in a healthy home. In time, we must release our grip on everything we hold dear.[3]

As You Are Left Behind

Steve and I suffered much the same as others. We mourned the loss of daily hugs, engaging conversations, the spontaneity of youthful humor, the instant parties when a gang of our children's friends popped in conveniently at mealtimes. But after the grief, after wandering through our children's rooms, hugging their stuffed animals, and studying every feature in their senior picture with sighs of longing, came a discovery as amazing as finding the key piece to a three-foot puzzle of the San Francisco skyline! It was a discovery that ushered months of lighthearted celebration into our lives and a heightened enjoyment of life.

Steve and I were on our own again after twenty-five years of dedicated, hearts-poured-into-it parenting, and it felt wonderful! We had a future together, just the two of us again. We were free to dream dreams, plan adventures, go fishing by ourselves, learn how to sail, write books, change careers, play the "oldies" loud, and eat the food we liked whenever we liked. Steve could now come home from work, put on his jogging clothes, and go for a run without having to solve "today's teen problems." And I could wear whatever I wanted when I greeted him at the door!

These were rich years with our children, but required sacrificing some of the richness of our time together as husband and wife. Now it had been given back—a gift from God which we accepted with great delight. Not only were our children free to become the adults God desired, but their parents entered the same freedom, as if in a dream, and it felt wonderful. There remained but one necessary step before the discoveries could be made.

LAYING IT DOWN

"I didn't do as well as I could have," confessed a friend recently as we talked, sipping steamy mugs of hot chocolate. "I could have done better, I know. I have to forgive myself." Looking across the table at the intense expression in her warm brown eyes, I thought, *What a wise and honest person she is.*

I'm not certain I'd trust a parent who thought he had done well and knew of nothing that needed forgiveness. Parenting, particularly the releasing part, is a humbling process. We come to the end of our wits so frequently, it's frightening. Gone are the "Father Knows Best" images we once thought to be reality. Instead, the daily need for wisdom, mercy, forgiveness, perspective, and good humor make us forge a well-worn path to our place of prayer. When I asked one of my son's favorite art teachers how his children were doing in college, he responded, "Fine, but my knees are worn out!" (Incidentally, this wonderful man teaches in public school! I applaud Christian teachers who remain on the front lines!)

There comes a point when we need to lay our parenting down in our Heavenly Father's lap: joys and sorrows, good moments and bad, hopes fulfilled and those delayed. It's His job now to finish what we began. We loved, drawing on His love when ours ran dry. We nursed, comforted, disciplined, taught, and led, unaware He was always there. Now, changed in the process, we bring our children back to God who trusted us with them in the first place. And we give them back, keenly aware we weren't all we wanted to be, and we weren't all our children needed. And He accepts them every time, as He accepts us every time we come.

As you lay down your parenting, God may remind you of some unfinished business with your spouse or one of your children—perhaps some unsettled anger or disappointment, words that wounded, emotional neglect, or an unfair judgment needing to be forgiven. Pursue the peace He offers by straightening out any unsettled accounts. If you aren't sure, ask your children, "Is there anything I have done in your growing-up years that hurt or offended you?" (Better sit down when you ask this.)

One of my daughters reminded me of a spanking she felt was undeserved. Looking back, I remembered vividly the morning when I lost my cool over her rather minimal defiance. She was absolutely right, and I asked her forgiveness.

In return, your adult children may ask your forgiveness for past offenses. It's a serendipitous blessing that follows clearing your own account when you hear confessions like, "Dad, remember that little streak of blue paint on the side of your new car? Well, I tried to rub it off when it happened, but I actually went around a curve too fast and hit a fence on someone's lawn. I'm truly sorry I never told you."

ALLOWING GOD FREEDOM

Once we have sincerely and prayerfully laid down our years of parenting in God's lap, it is necessary to trust that His choices are best, even if they are not what you would have chosen for your children. One mother continually resisted her daughter's pleas to change colleges, insisting that her father's choice for her was best. When I met her many years later, this mother still lamented that decision after it resulted in a lifetime of emotional distance between them.

As I look at the amazing people my own children are becoming, I realize I would have been wrong had I tried to make their choices of schools, career, or lifetime mate. Steve and I have learned to enjoy God's surprises; they are much more interesting than our own small plans. Accepting God's surprises means giving Him complete freedom to shape our children for the calling He will bring to their lives. Our part is to pray they will have a willing spirit when His direction comes and to let go with grace.

The following old poem is very moving as it tells of Zebedee, father of James and John, relating to his wife how he felt when Jesus called their sons to follow Him:

Zebedee's Sons

Salome! Had you been with me in the boat,
You would not chide and moan because our boys
Have gone with the Beloved from this our home.
Let me, Salome, tell you how it came.

The night was still—the tide was running strong,
Heavy our nets—the strain reached breaking point,
And while 'twas dark we docked, and as we worked
I felt as though new strength and steady joy
Surged through my being, so I sang a psalm—
As David sang—a song to greet the morn;
And then my heart was filled with quiet calm.

The boat was soon in order, and we turned
To dry and mend our nets. Then Jesus came—
He called the boys, first John, then James, by name,
And they arose and went to follow Him.

I turned and gazed on Jesus standing there—
He seemed to me all clothed in shining light
As He stood in the pathway with the night
Behind Him and the dawn breaking around,
His form so radiant and glad and free.

And when He climbed the hill our sons went too—
James was behind, and John was by His side;
And when they talked, John scarcely seemed our John—

I felt that he had caught a marvelous light.
And all my being seemed to overflow;
I knew the night had passed—the dawn had come,
And then I knew that we must let them go.[4]

As a new Christian on my first ladies' retreat, I once listened to an older woman describe her emotional struggle to release her son and daughter-in-law for missionary service in a distant part of the world. I didn't realize, as I do now, what her tears meant. Nor did this mother of preschoolers understand her joy when she decided to allow God freedom to direct her son's life according to His better plan. But now I am acquainted with both the tears and the joy and have found they are two hands with one heart.

"Those who sow in tears will reap with songs of joy" (Ps. 126:5) is a verse that has given me the urging I needed when trusting God meant an emotional tug-of-war. Parents who let go with tears will find a God who did too, and open their lives to multiplied joys.

CELEBRATING THE NEW YOU

Discovering New Freedom

Imagine in midlife becoming brand new! When I look in the mirror, I don't look brand new. I look cheerfully middle-aged. I don't even feel brand new. My doctor recently informed me that my joints are aging rather rapidly. (But she said it with a smile!) But on the inside, I'm becoming new every day.

I'm discovering new freedoms in my spirit, more generous thinking toward others, excitement over opportunities on the horizon, and a fresh willingness to learn and grow that I had allowed to tarnish during the busiest years of my life. If pushing fifty is more than halfway home, I want to enjoy every bit of my life from now on.

Central to every day's unfolding plan is celebrating all the small somethings that make up life, even if it's how good the morning coffee tastes or how brilliant the moon is at night.

PLUGGING HOLES IN THE EMPTY NEST

An empty nest doesn't need to be empty after all. It can be full of dreams and opportunities like these:

- ❖ Learn a new sport. Local clubs may provide low cost instruction and activities. Ask at shops that sell equipment for the sport you're interested in.
- ❖ Learn a new art or craft. Check with local colleges or craft shops for courses.
- ❖ Take up writing. There may be a writers' critique group in your area or a writer's conference nearby. Check with local colleges for information.
- ❖ Start a home business venture. But be sure to do your homework!
- ❖ Explore short-term mission work through your church or denomination.
- ❖ Enjoy your favorite foods without being teased.
- ❖ Organize old photos, tools, the attic, or garage.
- ❖ Make weekend plans on the spur of the moment.
- ❖ Volunteer to teach a class or serve on a committee at your church.
- ❖ Take a course together at a community college.
- ❖ Buy season tickets to a local college or pro team.
- ❖ Volunteer for a cause that interests you.
- ❖ Buy season tickets to the symphony, ballet, or theater.

- ❖ Remodel a room in your house.
- ❖ Update your landscaping.
- ❖ Plan your "dream home." It may even be the one you're living in now!

The freedom God gives us to become new is made clear in His Word: "Now the Lord is the Spirit, and where the Spirit of the Lord is, there is freedom. And we, who with unveiled faces all reflect the Lord's glory, are being transformed into His likeness with ever-increasing glory, which comes from the Lord, who is the Spirit" (2 Cor. 3:17–18). Who we become depends upon our acceptance of the changes and challenges God brings into our lives and how well we listen to God's directives. Jan Silvious, an encourager who has salted many lives through radio, speaking, and teaching, has this to say:

> Many people, by their mid-thirties, have stopped acquiring new skills and new attitudes in any aspect of their lives. In reality, there is much to be said for hanging onto the tried and true. If it works, why change? But much of life is unexperienced, so this may be the time in your life to give some new things a try. . . .
>
> The same principle applies in the spiritual realm as well. Caleb was a man who was unafraid of a challenge: "I was forty years old when Moses the servant of the LORD sent me from Kadesh Barnea to explore the land. And I brought him back a report according to my convictions, but my brothers who went up with me made the hearts of the people melt with fear. I, however, followed the LORD my God wholeheartedly" (Josh. 14:7–9).
>
> Many years later, we hear old Caleb saying, "Now, then, just as the LORD promised, he has kept me alive for forty-five years. . . . So here I am today, eighty-five years old! I am still as strong today as the day Moses sent me out; I'm just as vigorous to go out to battle now as I was then.

Now give me this hill country that the LORD promised me that day" (vv. 10–12).[5]

Caleb was no midlife couch potato! He began a difficult and challenging mission in life at a time when others were nestled in their recliners planning early retirement. A sense of excitement over God's purpose for his life kept him strong, positive, and vigorous. As we give God freedom to rebuild the tired, middle-aged person on the inside, a new you emerges, one that says, "What's next, Lord?" instead of "Bah, humbug!" That's something to celebrate!

Discovering New Ministries

Bill Hybels describes the joy of finding a new ministry: "When you're enjoying the fulfillment and fellowship that inevitably accompanies authentic service, ministry is a joy. Instead of exhausting you, it energizes you. Instead of burnout, you experience blessing. You say, 'It's a privilege. I want to do this for the rest of my life!' "[6]

God will never waste the lessons we've learned in these years of loving, launching, and letting go. One of the most meaningful ministries we could have once our children are on their own is cheering another family, or their young adult, through the same process. Every parent, regardless of his or her station in life, can become a friend and mentor to another. Parents whose children have recently left the nest are uniquely well equipped to reach out and encourage other parents who are bumping through the process themselves. What a wonderful time to offer a listening ear, a meal, or a "free weekend away" to an exhausted mom and dad.

A seasoned empty-nester and mother of five once shared this wisdom with me: "There are many solutions to a problem," she said, "but anything next to love is only second best." We can love by listening empathetically to other parents, praying for their children, and offering genuine friendship.

We don't have to counsel, just understand. We needn't solve their problems, just pray for solutions, and never, never criticize.

When Steve and I taught a parenting course at our church last year, we realized how few parents have someone to confide in, to ask about dating policies, challenges in family scheduling, parental differences in discipline. Where have all the role models gone? Sadly, many have gone back to work and are too busy to reach out to another parent struggling in midstream. How about you?

JUST THINKING

As you lay your years of parenting in your Heavenly Father's lap, ask Him for courage to seek forgiveness where it is needed. Choose a quiet time with your son or daughter alone, perhaps out for dinner together, and ask him if there are any unsettled hurts from his childhood. Two cautions: Never defend yourself. It's your son's or daughter's perceptions that matter—and be "all prayed up" before you attempt this. It will take a lot of honesty and humility.

On the positive side, drag out your dusty dreams some night in front of the fire, either alone or with your spouse. Write them down, adding any new dreams that have been waiting like wallflowers to be invited to dance again. Pick three of the best and ask God for three more you've never thought of. Let the excitement surge back into your life as you picture yourself fulfilling those dreams, becoming someone new, pursuing new challenges in His joyful strength. Then, like Caleb, move ahead to claim your "hill country"!

New beginnings: four ways to strengthen your marriage and your kids at the same time

Dad, that was great time! Two miles in less than fourteen minutes! Are you sure you're OK?" Dave panned the video camera the full length of Steve's prone body as he lay panting on the small patch of grass in front of the Voorheesville Fire Hall.

"Yea! I'm fine," he gasped. "Just winded. Get a picture of my watch." Dave zeroed in as Steve lifted a limp wrist.

"13 minutes and 56 seconds! That's awesome, Dad! You said you'd run in races before you were fifty and you did it! Say, you don't look too good! Are you *sure* you're all right? Here comes Mom and Lauren and Mike."

I got there first and knelt down, ready to administer CPR. "Steve, why are you on the ground? Are you breathing? Are you having chest pains?"

"He's fine, Mom. Just give him a minute to catch his breath." Lauren's calm assessment made me feel a little foolish.

"Good goin', big guy! I knew you could do it!" Mike's face widened into one of his famous dimpled grins.

Steve's first race was pretty impressive, I had to admit. All that working out for the past two years had really paid off. What impressed me most was his commitment. When Steve knew a goal was worth pursuing, he just wouldn't quit. Our kids are just the same.

Maintaining a healthy marriage long after the kids are gone is a worthy goal that will affect our children's happiness for many years, regardless of the effort it takes. Why? Because our success as marriage partners who place high value on our relationship and train to improve it will bring worlds of encouragement to our adult children as they launch out on their own. It may even be the reason they succeed.

Three of our four children are now happily married to people we love and admire. It gives us a lot of joy to watch them develop the skills that a good marriage requires. Recently Lauren called to share her thoughts for this chapter, "Mom, make sure you tell parents that what they do after the kids leave is really important. We are really affected by the way you live your lives."

"What do you mean, honey?" I asked.

"I mean the way you and Dad keep growing together, learning new things, branching out, and the way you love each other so much and do so many fun things together now. You're never boring. It makes us want to live like that, too. It helps us not give up when things get tough. You two didn't."

I felt honored by her words. Each of our children has shared similar thoughts with us. But there were times when we both came close to throwing in the towel. The stresses involved with raising and launching a big family drain a person until there's little left to give, especially to one another. Creating a joyful and fulfilling marriage took major commitment and hard work, but it was actually a surprisingly simple process with great rewards along the way.

FOUR WAYS TO BEGIN AGAIN

1. Put a Marker in the Ground

As every runner knows, the race has got to start some-where, and rebuilding a tired marriage is no different. Make a decision that, from this day on, you will move forward, never back. Chuck Swindoll, in his uplifting and honest book, *Laugh Again,* has this to say: "In this race called life, we are to face forward, anticipating what lies ahead, ever stretching and reaching, making life a passionate, adventurous quest. Life was never meant to be a passive coexistence with enemy forces as we await our heavenly home. But it's easy to do that, especially when we arrive at a certain age. . . to sort of shift into neutral and take whatever comes our way."[1]

Putting a marker in the ground means refusing to let go of the lifetime commitment you made on your wedding day. It means being willing to stretch and reach hard for a life together that's better than anything you've previously known. To get started, most of us have to shake ourselves out of a passive mindset. A little incident helped me see my own tendency to settle for second best.

I came home from shopping one Saturday last spring and held up a new bathing suit. It happened that Dave was home for the weekend, and he and Steve both looked up and just stared for about ten seconds without comment at my new suit.

"Well, don't you like it? I thought you'd like the bright flowers. I got it on sale."

"It's very nice," Steve said politely, not wanting to offend me.

Dave, knowing he was leaving soon anyway, said, "I'd take it back. It looks like a 'settle for' bathing suit. Is it really the kind you wanted, Mom?"

"Well, no, but it covers me up well, and the colors are my favorite, and it was 30 percent off. But . . . looking at it again,

I guess it is a 'settle for' suit." I'm ashamed to admit I never took it back. Every time I wear it, I feel like a flowered blob.

Our attitude toward marriage can be much like my attitude toward that bathing suit. Do you really want a "settle for" marriage? Do you have the courage and commitment it takes to go for the best there is? If so, your conditioning will mean giving 100 percent all the time. Dennis Rainey in his book *Lonely Husbands, Lonely Wives* contrasts this with the world's "50/50 Plan":

> The biblical plan for marriage states, "I will do everything I can to love you, without demanding 'an equal amount' in return." This is a 100/100 Plan of unconditional acceptance, which builds oneness instead of isolation. . . .
>
> If marriages are to succeed and become havens of oneness rather than dungeons of isolation, Christians must do more than simply "add a few Christian touches" to the world's 50/50 Plan. The 100/100 Plan calls for a total change of mind and heart, a total commitment to God and one another. This is the plan, the super glue, that holds a marriage together no matter what pressures may come.[2]

Adopting the "100/100 Plan" takes only minutes of decision making, but putting it into practice takes patience, time, unselfishness, and the courage to make critical choices.

2. Get on Each Other's Team

Steve and I frequently hear couples say, "We'd really like to spend more quality time together, but there just isn't any. We're both so busy with our jobs, we're hardly home at the same time, and when we are, we're exhausted." How many couples are willing to let ambitious career goals rest even a few years while they are raising their children or rebuilding a relationship of lifetime importance with their spouse?

When our children were growing up, Steve was faced with the constant pressure to publish research in professional journals in order to maintain an edge in academics. It meant stepping off a faster career track and possibly remaining at the same level for years, but he reached a decision one day that having time available to our growing family was a higher value than his career. God honored that decision in the long run, and Steve now has both the love and respect of his family and the high esteem of his colleagues in education.

Similarly, I chose to postpone graduate work and teaching in order to be at home to raise our children. But it was an easy choice. I was never the dyed-in-the-wool student Steve was. Although I have done part-time teaching and private tutoring for years, my goals have changed to writing and speaking. I'm thankful I didn't sacrifice those priceless years with my children for a career I would not have found as fulfilling as this.

Husbands and wives are partners in the race called "life." When our marriage is limping along, suffering from too little attention during the child-launching years, it's time to make a choice. We either slow our pace and attend to the relationship with the tenderness and 100 percent commitment our mate deserves, or we let our marriage drop, wounded, by the wayside. The difficulties mount quickly when we realize this is a high stakes race. Our grown children are watching us run, and their video cameras are running. If we fail to finish, will they have the courage to run well themselves?

TEAM-MATES

Husbands and wives who choose to get on each other's team, rather than pull in opposite directions, will never cripple one another with criticism, nagging, and complaining. That's being a lousy sport in any game. A good teammate will:

❖ obey all the rules
❖ stoop to lift the other when he's hurting

❖ become his best encourager

❖ choose to see the good and overlook the bad

❖ want his or her mate to win more than himself

❖ do everything possible to honor his partner and make him or her look good

❖ choose to put his or her mate first ahead of job, church, personal plans, even children

❖ celebrate his partner's success.

If this describes your marriage relationship, your team is bound to win.

---

3. Practice the "3 Rs"

Choosing to make your marriage a top priority begins with a calendar and a pen. Remember the days when there were just the two of you? Once a week, make a date with your mate you'd rather die than break. Label it your private "3 Rs," or "Relax, Respond, and Rediscover." Steve and I have made a career out of finding creative ways to do just that. Let me give you a few ideas:

Relax. Leave your watch at home, turn on the answering machine, and don't bring home a pile of papers from the office on the night you reserve for each other.

Husbands, remember how you once won her heart? Pull out all the stops, bring her flowers or cashews or whatever makes her feel special. Steve knows I get warm fuzzies over cheddar cheese popcorn. For my sister-in-law, Cindy, it's double-dipped chocolate mints.

Wives, a part of your past that's good to revisit is how to look and behave like a girlfriend. Help your husband plan a restful afternoon or evening you'd both enjoy—alone. Date nights are just for the two of you. Friends are one notch lower on the priority list. Conversation topics to nix are the children, problems at work, and diets. Everything else pleasant and positive is fair game.

We've had some great dates doing conventional things like going out for dinner, watching an *uplifting* movie, window-shopping at the mall, then stopping for a cappucino and dessert. But we also love the unconventional, like paddling around a quiet pond in our canoe with our fishing rods and a picnic lunch. Once we thought a dragon was following us on a long hike in the woods and looked up to see people waving out of a hot air balloon about twenty feet above our heads. We have friends who put on their comfortable old jeans and drive into the mountains and go antique hunting or simply sniff out a new adventure.

Respond. Learning to respond lovingly to one another, to share our innermost thoughts and feelings, is a skill that takes time to train. It also requires safety—safety from criticism, any form of ridicule or sarcasm, and the understanding that confidences shared will never be repeated.

"Everyone should be quick to listen, slow to speak and slow to become angry," the Bible says (James 1:19). It's the most unnatural thing in the world to do. Without the Holy Spirit's power to respond first to God, and then to our mate, we remain naturally self-centered, outspoken, and critical. Yet, when Jesus Christ lives in our heart, and we commit our will to Him, He enables us, through His strength and love, to obey His clear directives: to "live a life worthy of the calling you have received. Be completely humble and gentle; be patient, bearing with one another in love" (Eph. 4:1–2).

Would your marriage and mine be worthy of cheering on if we lived the kind of love these verses describe? "Love is patient, love is kind. It does not envy, it does not boast, it is not proud. It is not rude, it is not self-seeking, it is not easily angered, it keeps no record of wrongs. Love does not delight in evil but rejoices with the truth. It always protects, always trusts, always hopes, always perseveres. Love never fails" (1 Cor. 13:4–8).

Responding lovingly is an art form rarely observed. It means listening to one another with intensity, focusing entirely on understanding your spouse rather than expressing your own opinion. It means returning words that lift and soothe and mend. It is loving like Jesus does.

Rediscover fun. "The characteristic of love is spontaneity," Oswald Chambers reflected. "The springs of love are in God, not in us . . . . The evidence of our love for Him is the absolute spontaneity of our love, it comes naturally."[3] Some of the best love gifts are unplanned, fragrant with affection, and very extravagant. I received such a gift last winter.

Steve had gone outside to bring in firewood one evening following a huge winter snowstorm that buried our area under more than a foot of fresh snow. I had wandered around the house all weekend in my robe, nursing a bad cold and feeling terrible. I knew I looked dreadful.

Suddenly, a loud banging on the family room window made me jump! There was Steve looking like the abominable snowman, beaming and motioning for me to come and look at the ground. Turning on the outside floodlight, I looked, and there was the biggest, most perfect snow angel I'd ever seen! Just like the ones I used to make as a little girl! Steve stood next to it looking so proud of himself. What a spontaneous love gift for a pathetic-looking, sick wife. It made me feel totally loved!

Rediscovering the fun you once loved as a child, or dreamed of as a young adult, brings energy, laughter, and hilarity back into your life. It's a way to celebrate life after the kids leave home. Listen to the surprise Bill Hybels had one day:

One afternoon, shortly after we were married, Lynne and I heard a noisy commotion in our front yard. We ran out and found a big, custom-painted Harley Davidson motorcycle with two riders in black leather jackets and big black helmets with tinted visors that covered their faces. They had driven right up on our sidewalk, and the driver was revving the engine as high as possible. Finally, the rider on the back slid off, removed her helmet—and it was Lynne's mother!

Here was my demure mother-in-law, and my hardworking father-in-law sitting on a motorcycle in the middle of my sidewalk! They had ridden over from Michigan to surprise us.

I was shocked. I was speechless.

Finally Lynne said, "Relax, Bill. It's no big deal. They do things like this all the time."[4]

When I first read this story, I thought of Chuck Swindoll and his wife, Cynthia, pulling up on their new Harley! It would be hard to be bored in a marriage that made it a mission to rediscover fun. But most important is the message it sends to our adult children that a great marriage is a lifetime investment of love and is worth every effort it takes to make it wonderful.

As a newly married man, Bill was challenged by his in-laws' marriage. "It was so obvious that after decades of marriage they were still madly in love with one another. Finally I learned the secret of their success: 'They do things like this all the time.'"

For years Steve and I nearly forgot how to have fun. Life was serious business with tight schedules, job stresses, and teenagers with problems. Even though we had always made an effort at keeping a regular "date night," we were often too tired or too stressed to relax and have fun. One of the people whose writing did the most to lift us out of our slump was Barbara Johnson. I marveled at her deliberate decision to "choose joy" in the midst of sorrow and stress. I found her books rich collections of encouragement, wise advice, and lots of chuckles. She credits learning to laugh again with her returned strength and joy:

> Doctors and physical fitness experts tell us that laughter is just plain good for your health. . . . One medical doctor . . . calls laughter "internal jogging." He says that hearty laughter has a beneficial effect on most of your body's systems—and it's a lot more fun than calisthenics. Laughing 100 times a day works the heart as much as exercising for ten minutes on a rowing machine. . . .
>
> Have you ever thought of how many days we waste if we don't learn to laugh? . . . There are so many books out on how to love your family, how to succeed in marriage, how to get thin, how to get rich, how to cope, how to survive an earthquake, what to do when teenagers run away from home, but nothing on how to learn to laugh. How often parents are told to "zip up your child and give the entire container to the Lord because there is no way out of this." But parents need to hear God can take them through whatever they're facing. And learning to laugh can make the journey so much more comfortable![5]

So join me in jogging on the inside. Choose joy, learn to laugh again, decide to rediscover fun! Let's face it, the alternative is becoming a regular bore.

4. Share a Vision

Midlife sometimes acts like a magnifying glass. It reduces our view to the vast importance of small things like a child's questions, hugs, personal notes in the mail, the smells of things we love. Strangely true as well, we see the bigger picture of life more accurately now than even a few years ago, the family heritage, a sense of calling and purpose, the breadth of God's love, and our deep unworthiness. It is a time of contrasts, a time for reevaluation of priorities, and an open window for change.

Throughout the years of child rearing—particularly the strenuous launching years—God has gotten our undivided attention many times. We've needed Him, begged Him to help our children, and received His answers. And now we are changed and grateful. We hear His still, small voice asking for *our help* now. God whispers His concern for His children who aren't safely home yet, who are struggling, who need someone to tell them of His unchanging love, to extend His arm of comfort, His Word of counsel, His message of hope and encouragement. Who will reach them? Who will stand in the gap; who will give of themselves; who will pray and love on His behalf? Why not me? Why not you?

The greatest joy a couple can have in a renewed marriage is sharing a vision for God's purpose for their remaining years together. Our training has been unique, like no one else's. We have been tested, brought low, qualified, groomed. And now it's our turn to stand strong. The Scriptures call it serving "shoulder to shoulder" with the Lord (Zeph. 3:9).

How does God reveal His purpose? Sometimes He puts a longing in your heart, like this young couple the Swindolls met:

> Cynthia and I recently had lunch with a wonderful couple in their thirties who are seriously considering a mid-career change. He will go to seminary and she will go to work to put him through. They have been thinking about it for years. Both are so excited, so motivated. They said we were the first ones to sound enthusiastic; all the others they had mentioned this to were quick to point out all the possible things that could go wrong. All the sacrifices they would have to endure. Why focus on that? I told them to keep reaching forward . . . to pursue their dream. And do I need to mention it? Both were laughing again as they walked away.[6]

Other times, God puts people nearby who need encouragement. His requests are often so small as to seem not quite big enough to be "God's work": making time for coffee with a friend, a daily phone chat with a teenager, working on an old car with the son of a single mom. Depending on your spiritual gifts and your readiness to serve, you may fill a need for a teacher, a small group or youth leader, a ministry position, or offer your home to host a prayer group or Bible study.

Every service done "shoulder to shoulder" with Jesus, regardless of how big or small, will bring joy and a sense of shared vision as a couple. Your marriage will be enhanced and strengthened, for "a cord of three strands is not quickly broken" (Eccl. 4:12). And your watching children will put their own marker in the ground.

JUST THINKING

Why not take out your calendar and pen, sit down with your spouse, and make a date this week? Then make one for next week, and the week after. Commit yourselves to finding creative ways to relax, respond to one another in love, and rediscover fun once again.

Remembering you are in training together, talk about how well you are both pulling in the same direction. What ways could you better act as teammates? What changes are you willing to make in order to reach the goal?

Single parents, do you know couples whose marriages are good examples to your children? Thank them sometime for making the effort. Explain to your young adult that great marriages don't just happen. They take lots of teamwork.

᠌

CHAPTER THIRTEEN

You look just like your Father: raising kids who warm God's heart

*L*auren, isn't there some way we could drive up this hill?" I groaned, following my daughter's determined strides up the steep, curved driveway to the Holiday Inn parking lot.

"No, silly, the car's parked at the top! You won't believe the view of Mirror Lake once you reach the top. It's breathtaking!"

"It's breathtaking just getting there! I've got to stop and rest a minute. You have lupus! Why are you able to climb this tortuous hill and I'm having so much trouble?" I looked up at my tall, blonde daughter smiling down at me and wondered where she got the resolve and physical strength to attempt such a climb, when many days, for her, simply getting out of bed was a challenge.

"I guess I feel pretty good today, Mom. Come on, let's go. We're almost at the top. You can make it!" As Lauren reached out a hand to help me, I was struck by the picture of the generational effect of parenting. Here was my daughter helping me, encouraging me, leading me as I had once led her. I remembered being asked about a year before in an interview, who my heroes were. A truth welled up, as it did now: My heroes are my children.

How did Lauren become this godly young woman? Where did Amy tap the source of her inner beauty? What hand plumbed the depth of David's strength and compassion, or forged Bob's perseverance and surprising gentleness? We did not produce these qualities in our children, but we led them to the One who could.

Whose Likeness Is This?

I have often thought of the Bible as God's family scrapbook. In it He records the stories of His children—the ones who did well and also those who didn't. I picture Him turning the pages for me, saying, "Take a look at my son Abraham. The night he offered Isaac, all of heaven held its breath. I knew I had the right man. And Joseph, oh precious Joseph! How faithful he was over every little thing! I rewarded him with his heart's desires and gave him charge over all of Egypt. Now take a look at Moses. Moses was a little hard to work with at first, but he came around after all those years in the wilderness. They usually do." And on and on throughout the Scriptures—Daniel, David, Nehemiah, Esther, Joshua, Paul, Peter, Stephen, Mark, Barnabas, John—God unfolds the history of His children on this earth who were shaped into His likeness through the heat of testing and the miracle of believing.

God's heart yearns for His children to become image-bearers, "blameless and pure, children of God without fault in a crooked and depraved generation, in which you shine like stars in the universe as you hold out the word of life" (Phil. 2:15–16). The great legacy of the Christian home is bearing the family likeness of Christ to the next generation.

King David, humbled by grace and forgiveness, rejoiced in being given "the heritage of those who fear your name"

(Ps. 61:5). When we warm our Heavenly Father's heart by faithfully bearing His image and releasing children who do the same, we share in the same heritage as David. This, I believe, is our most important purpose in parenting.

What can parents do to encourage a Christlike character in their young adults when it matters most, as they are ready to leave the nest? Like climbing alone into the cockpit of an airplane, our children's faith and character are about to be tested like never before. Mom and Dad have to stay behind, but they can have the assurance that their children are well equipped for the flight and are never really alone. God is in the cockpit with them. Equipping them for the journey means training for character and faith, modeling it at home, fanning the flames of Christlikeness and giving your blessing of affirmation. If your young adult has not yet left home, there is still time to improve on all four.

Preparing Your Children for Life

Training for Character and Faith

We assume so much as parents. We assume our children will know how to make good decisions, learn what to do when in doubt, and know how to lead a balanced life. The reality is those skills need to be taught before they ever leave home.

Steve was wonderful with our teens the way he led family devotions in his humorous, unpreachy way. He endured loads of good-natured joking and ridicule whenever he came home with one of his famous gray posters.

"Oh, Dad!" our teenagers groaned. "Not another one of these! What cute little saying is it this time?"

And Steve would whip out the back of a legal pad and hold it up at the dinner table with a smile like the Cheshire cat. "You'll love it! This one is great. I thought of it at work today, now listen up!" And so began another "life lesson" that hit the nail on the head every time and is remembered by our adult children to this day. Here are a few we considered best:

❖ Teenage life is electric with choices laden with lifetime consequences. Steve taught our kids, "When in doubt, DRAFT it! (Do Right And Feel Terrific!)" It's amazing how often that simple message has spoken at just the right moment to caution against danger or encourage responsible actions. It works for parents, too.

❖ The hardest thing for parents to do is step back and let their young adults make big decisions on their own. Steve explained to our teens how decisions reveal character and spring from our faith and values. Then he gave them "Five Steps to Making a Good Decision":

1. Accept the challenge. Don't avoid making a decision. It's God's way of saying, "You're mature enough to handle this."

2. Search for alternatives. This includes asking for advice. Do you have all the necessary information? Is there a better way to approach this problem? How have those you respect handled similar situations?

3. Search for biblical truth or faith-based alternatives through prayer. Ask for God's help and read His Word, looking for direct instruction or principles that apply. Don't hurry this.

4. Become committed to one biblical alternative. When you feel you have the course of action that agrees with Scripture, is confirmed by the advice of those you respect, and gives you peace in your heart, commit yourself to it.

5. Stick with the decision. Don't be a "double-minded man, unstable in all he does" (James 1:8). Second-guessers, in other words, become miserable people who accomplish very little in life and have peace about nothing. When you make a decision the right way, you can usually live with it.

❖ By far our favorite acrostic was RTOPA (pronounced "R-T-OPA"). Inspired by a famous droid, R2D2 of *Star Wars* fame, RTOPA was easy to remember and aimed at teaching a balanced life. The letters stood for "Read, Trust, Obey, Pray, and Act," and were balanced like a seesaw over a fulcrum with Truth on one side and Love on the other. It means as we read, trust, and obey God's Word, it will lead to prayerful actions on our part that glorify God. The balance hits at the point of our obedience to God.

In every life, the point of positive change begins in the will. Jesus linked His family likeness with our will when He said, "Whoever does God's will is my brother and sister and mother" (Mark 3:35).

Modeling Christlikeness

Throughout this book much has been said about the importance of modeling the Christlike life in a winsome way. Rather than repeat the same principles, suffice it to say that every lesson we hope to teach begins first with us as parents. Hypocrisy destroys faith, but authenticity is the aroma that makes us hunger after godliness. If a young person finds it at home, he is wealthier than most.

Oswald Chambers spoke to himself, as well, when he said, "I am called to live in perfect relation to God so that my life produces a longing after God in other lives, not admiration for myself."[1] In no way do we want our children to become parent worshipers, thinking we are the perfect role models. That's a prelude to major disillusionment the first time we let them down. But we can demonstrate a continual moving forward in our own walk with God and a heart that's eager to obey Him. That's authenticity.

Parents are, after all, still children in the process of growing up. God addresses us as such in Ephesians 5:1–2: "Be imitators of God, therefore, as dearly loved children and live a life of love, just as Christ loved us and gave himself up for us as a fragrant offering and sacrifice to God." What a model for parents to follow! When we aim to live and love as Jesus does, we will see His reflection in our young adults.

Fanning the Flame

In the process of loving, launching, and letting go, there are moments to celebrate along the way. Every child has these moments, even strugglers. When your son or daughter does something so right, so caring and generous, so loving or forgiving that you need to stop and just look at him, amazed, that's cause for a celebration. Even if it's tiny, fan the flame of goodness, encourage generosity, leap for joy when faith wins over doubt, frame the moments God prizes. Tell your son or daughter, "It's just like you to be the one who was kind (or whatever he did). I always knew you were very special."

My friend Brenda told me about a moment she celebrated with her fifteen-year-old son recently. He had been struggling under the weight of excessive homework loads and feeling worn out and exhausted. Brenda and her husband were concerned that the private school he attended was far too demanding. Would he get discouraged and give up? She went into his room one night as he studied and said, "Honey, maybe you should consider transferring to public school. This seems so hard. You don't have any time to yourself anymore."

He looked up at her, incredulous, "Mom, I can't. You don't understand; this school is my ministry. I belong here. God is using me here to be a witness. I can't quit just because it's hard."

Brenda's eyes filled with tears as she looked at this son who was more a man than she knew. "When I was a teenager," she confided to me later, "all I thought about was myself: my plans, my hair, who liked me, what boys I liked. My son is more concerned about others than he is for himself. I'm so proud of him!"

Moments like these may highlight your son's or daughter's emerging spiritual gifts. Like windows opened to their soul, parents can peer in and marvel at the symmetry and beauty God is building there. Make the most of every opportunity to affirm your teen or young adult as his life reflects the image of God within.

THE FATHER'S LIKENESS

How will you recognize when your children are becoming the kind of people God intends? Watch for qualities like these and their indicators:

* Truthfulness—Maintaining a clear conscience, even when it makes them look bad.

* Integrity—Doing the right thing when no one is looking; keeping their word.

* Humility—Willingness to take advice; a lack of arrogance or conceit over accomplishments; not having to have the "last word."

* Patience—Taking time for others who need time; willing to wait for things to happen.

* Perseverance—Staying with a task until it is completed, especially when it's frustrating or difficult; exercising self-control.

* Generosity—Looking for ways to refresh others, kindness evidenced by sharing of time, talent, and resources.

❖ A Servant Spirit—Willingness to meet others' needs, even when it's inconvenient.

❖ Loving kindness—Being understanding and compassionate toward others; affectionate and expressive in meaningful ways.

❖ Gratefulness—Learning to look for God's goodness in life; seldom self-centered or discouraged; not demanding.

❖ Prayerfulness—Carrying others' burdens in prayer; learning to view prayer as central to life; seldom anxious or fretful.

❖ Forgiving—Approachable; doesn't hold a grudge, is able to let go of past hurts.

Giving a Blessing

Affirming even the briefest moment that a young adult displays a Christlike character encourages him or her more than we realize. A parent's spoken blessing is tremendously powerful and can build strength that lasts a lifetime and even offer direction for a young life. Words like these make a real difference: "You have such a tender heart toward less fortunate people. I wonder how God is going to use all the gentleness you show?" or "Our house is such a happy place when you're home! I think it's because you are so caring toward others. You're never self-centered."

Gary Smalley and John Trent have done a remarkable job explaining this principle in their book *The Gift of the Blessing.* Every parent will thank himself for reading it, particularly those whose parents never spoke words of blessing to him. For parents who find verbal expression awkward or uncomfortable, Smalley and Trent write about another form of blessing:

Written words become a lifelong legacy for a child to keep. In a letter, you can express your pride in them, or share what you're learning from the Scriptures, or what you're doing that fills them in on your life. Whether they're waiting in the mail-line in the military, reaching into their mailbox at school, or thumbing through their letters in their own home or apartment, written words of blessing from a parent are incredibly powerful.[2]

Some of us have saved letters from our parents written twenty, thirty, even fifty years ago. That says volumes about the value of written affirmation. In response, I am committed to writing more notes and letters to my children and their spouses, to our parents, as well as others who have made a real difference in our lives, while there is still time.

TOUCHING THE FUTURE

Raising a generation of difference-makers, of children whose lives are stamped with the reality of God, will do more to advance the cause of Christ in this world than a hundred books written on the subject. Our children will touch the future; they will go where we cannot; they will dream dreams God has never given to us; they will love those we may never know; they will succeed where we have only begun. They are the true salt of the earth—God's image-bearers to the next generation.

Gordon and Gail MacDonald were image-bearers for Steve and me as new Christians and young parents. We were nurtured by their teaching, warmed by their friendship, and discipled by them without even knowing it. No doubt, Gordon and Gail prayed us into a life that wanted more than anything to bear His image, too.

Gordon reflects on the feelings of being "all done" as parents in a sentimental and thoughtful account of their life as a family in his book *There's No Place Like Home*. From another parent who has witnessed God's amazing workings in his children's lives and his own, comes this prayer:

> I have this prayer for men and women who are in the midst of the people-building process in the home right now. I pray for their delight in what they do. For their resiliency when things go awry. For their grace when the youngsters fail. For positive outside influences and mentors where a mother lacks the partnership of a father. For daily awareness that they build their children in cooperation with and dependence on God. For good school teachers who will care. For churches who will make ministry to children and youth a priority. For opportunities to talk, to work together, to play, to kiss, to cheer one another on. [3]

I have taken great delight being your cheerleader in this book. It is my prayer that your children will become your heroes, too—image-bearers with their parents, born to carry the reality of the love of God to the next generation.

JUST THINKING

One evening take time with the young adults in your home and review the "five steps to making a good decision." Use an example from your own life, and discuss any current decisions your son or daughter is working on. Plant a few wisdom seeds with Steve's little acrostics, DRAFT it and RTOPA. Have fun with them.

More important, watch for those wisdom seeds to sprout. Be alert for your son's or daughter's spiritual gifts. Plant a blessing in his heart with words of affirmation and love that will yield manyfold in years to come.

Suggested reading

Burkett, Larry. *Using Your Money Wisely*. Chicago: Moody Press, 1985.

Campbell, Ross. *How to Really Love Your Teenager*. Wheaton, Ill.: Victor, 1981.

Chapian, Marie. *Mothers and Daughters*. Minneapolis: Bethany House, 1988.

Covey, Stephen R. *The 7 Habits of Highly Effective People*. New York: Simon & Schuster, 1989.

Dobson, James. *Children at Risk*. Dallas: Word, 1990.

———. *Dr. Dobson Answers Your Questions About Raising Children*. Wheaton: Tyndale House, 1982.

———. *Parenting Isn't for Cowards*. Dallas: Word, 1987.

Heavilin, Marilyn Willett. *When Your Dreams Die*. Nashville, Tenn.: Here's Life Publishers, 1990.

Hybels, Bill. *Honest to God?* Grand Rapids: Zondervan, 1990.

Johnson, Barbara. *Fresh Elastic for Stretched Out Moms*. Old Tappan, N.J.: Fleming H. Revell Co., 1986.

————. *So Stick a Geranium in Your Hat and Be Happy!* Dallas: Word, 1990.

Kuykendall, Carol. *Give Them Wings.* Colorado Springs: Focus on the Family, 1994.

LaHaye, Beverly. *Prayer: God's Comfort for Today's Family.* Nashville, Tenn.: Thomas Nelson Publishers, 1990.

Lewis, Paul. *Forty Ways to Teach Your Child Values.* Wheaton: Tyndale, 1986.

MacDonald, Gordon. *There's No Place Like Home.* Wheaton: Tyndale, 1990.

McDowell, Josh. *Right from Wrong.* Dallas: Word, 1994.

Sanders, Bill. *Almost Everything Teens Want Parents to Know but Are Afraid to Tell Them.* Old Tappan, N.J.: Fleming H. Revell Co., 1987.

Silvious, Jan. *Please Don't Say You Need Me.* Grand Rapids: Zondervan, 1989.

Smalley, Gary and John Trent. *The Gift of the Blessing.* Nashville: Thomas Nelson Publishers, 1993.

Strommen, Merton P. and A. Irene. *Five Cries of Parents.* New York: Harper & Row, 1985.

Wilkerson, David. *The Jesus Person Pocket Promise Book.* Ventura, Calif.: Regal Books, 1972.

❧

Notes

Chapter Two

1. *Webster's Third New International Dictionary Unabridged* (Springfield, Mass.: Merriam-Webster Inc.,1986).

2. Oswald Chambers, *My Utmost for His Highest* (New York: Dodd, Mead & Co., 1935), 214.

Chapter Three

1. Poem by Annie Johnson Flint taken from Mrs. Charles E. Cowman, *Springs in the Valley* (Grand Rapids: Cowman Publications and Daybreak Books, 1939, 1968), 202–203.

2. Elisa Morgan, *I'm Tired of Waiting* (Wheaton, Ill.: Victor Books, 1989), 92–93.

3. Merton P. and A. Irene Strommen, *Five Cries of Parents* (San Francisco: Harper and Row Publishers, 1985), 35.

4. Ruth Bell Graham, *Sitting by My Laughing Fire* (Waco, Texas: Word Books, 1977), 159.

Chapter Four

1. Barbara Johnson, *Fresh Elastic for Stretched Out Moms* (Old Tappan, N.J.: Fleming H. Revell Co., 1986), 69.

2. Ramona Cramer Tucker, "Twila Paris: Home for the Holidays," *Today's Christian Woman* (November/December 1994), 59.

3. David Augsburger, *Caring Enough to Be Heard* (Ventura, Calif.: Regal Books, 1982), 11–12.

4. Stephen R. Covey, *The 7 Habits of Highly Effective People* (New York: Simon & Schuster, 1989), 240.

5. Tucker, "Twila Paris," 59.

Chapter Five

1. Carol Kuykendall, *Give Them Wings* (Colorado Springs: Focus on the Family, 1994), 166–67.

2. Larry Burkett, *Using Your Money Wisely* (Chicago: Moody Press, 1985), 192.

Chapter Six

1. William J. Bennett, *The Book of Virtues* (New York: Simon & Schuster, 1993), 11.

2. Bill Hybels, *Honest to God?* (Grand Rapids: Zondervan, 1990), 89–90.

3. Ann Landers, *The Daily Gazette*, September 9, 1994. Permission granted by Ann Landers and Creators Syndicate.

Chapter Seven

1. Gary Smalley, *The Key to Your Child's Heart* (Waco, Texas: Word Books, 1984), 49.

2. Bill Sanders, *Almost Everything Teens Want Parents to Know* (Old Tappan, N. J.: Fleming H. Revell Co., 1987), 25–26.

3. Jan Silvious, *Please Don't Say You Need Me* (Grand Rapids: Zondervan Publishing House, 1989), 55–56.

4. Oswald Chambers, *Oswald Chambers: The Best from All His Books,* ed. Harry Verploegh, vol. 1 (Nashville, Tenn.: Thomas Nelson Publishers, 1987), 310.

5. Terry Beck, "Can You Grow Peaches on an Almond Tree?" *Parents of Teenagers,* September/October 1993, 54.

Chapter Eight

1. Carole Feldman, "Student Cheating Admitted," *The Gazette,* October 20, 1993.

2. Zig Ziglar, *Raising Positive Kids in a Negative World* (Nashville, Tenn.: Oliver Nelson Books, 1985), 165.

3. Josh McDowell, *Right from Wrong* (Dallas: Word, 1994), 125–26.

4. Margie Lewis with Gregg Lewis, *The Hurting Parent,* rev. and exp. ed. (Grand Rapids: Zondervan Books, 1988), 92.

5. Ibid., 93.

6. McDowell, 200.

Chapter Nine

1. "I Will Change Your Name," words and music by D.J. Butler, used with permission of Mercy Publishing, 1987.

2. Jeffrey T. Jernigan, "Failure: One of Life's Best Teachers," *Decision,* September 1993, 27.

3. A. B. Davidson, "Strength Renewed," *Decision,* June 1994, 34.

4. Ruth Bell Graham, *Sitting by My Laughing Fire* (Waco, Tex.: Word Books, 1977), 36.

5. Barbara Johnson, *So Stick a Geranium in Your Hat and Be Happy!* (Dallas: Word Publishing, 1990), 84.

6. Bill Hybels, *Who You Are (When No One's Looking)* (Downers Grove, Ill.: Intervarsity Press, 1987), 71.

Chapter Ten

1. Bill Hybels, *Who You Are (When No One's Looking)* (Downers Grove, Ill.: Intervarsity Press, 1987), 71.

2. Cliff Barrows, "A Conversation with My Dad," *Decision,* June 1994, 15.

3. Barbara Johnson, *Fresh Elastic for Stretched Out Moms* (Old Tappan, N.J.: Fleming H. Revell Company, 1986), 78.

Chapter Eleven

1. Ruth Bell Graham, *Sitting by My Laughing Fire* (Waco, Tex.: Word Books, 1977), 117.

2. Marie Chapian, *Mothers and Daughters* (Minneapolis: Bethany House, 1988), 173–74.

3. James C. Dobson, Focus on the Family letter, July 1989. Quoted in Carol Kuykendall, *Give Them Wings* (Colorado Springs: Focus on the Family, 1994), 144.

4. Mrs. Charles E. Cowman, *Springs in the Valley* (Grand Rapids: Cowman Publications and Daybreak Books, 1939, 1968), 292.

5. Jan Silvious, *The Five-Minute Devotional* (Grand Rapids: Zondervan, 1991), 181.

6. Bill Hybels, *Honest to God?* (Grand Rapids: Zondervan, 1990), 117.

Chapter Twelve

1. Charles R. Swindoll, *Laugh Again* (Dallas: Word, 1992), 148.

2. Dennis Rainey, *Lonely Husbands, Lonely Wives* (Dallas: Word, 1989), 54.

3. Oswald Chambers, *My Utmost for His Highest* (New York: Dodd, Mead and Co., 1935), 121.

4. Bill Hybels, *Honest to God?* (Grand Rapids: Zondervan, 1990), 77–78.

5. Barbara Johnson, *So Stick a Geranium in Your Hat and Be Happy!* (Dallas: Word, 1990), 72–73.

6. Swindoll, 149–50.

Chapter Thirteen

1. Oswald Chambers, *My Utmost for His Highest* (New York: Dodd, Mead and Co., 1935), 337.

2. Gary Smalley and John Trent, *The Gift of the Blessing* (Nashville, Tenn.: Thomas Nelson Publishers,1993), 225.

3. Gordon MacDonald, *There's No Place Like Home* (Wheaton, Ill.: Tyndale House, 1990), 305.